THE BLACKEST BLUE

S.D. EPPS

THE BLACKEST BLUE

Autobigraphical Novel Written by: S. D. Epps

Cover Illustration Copyright © 2023 by Nisha Yolanda

Cover design by Nisha Yolanda

Novel design and production by: Nisha Yolanda

Editing by :S.D. Epps

Publishing: Efesee Corporation

Photographs: Courtesy of S.D. Epps

Author photograph: S.D. Epps

THE BLACKEST BLUE

Disclaimer

The following disclaimer is provided for the autobiographical novel titled The Blackest Blue. Please read this disclaimer carefully before proceeding with the content of the book.

Personal Experiences and Perspectives

The Blackest Blue is a work of non-fiction based on the personal experiences and perspectives of the author. The events, narratives, and interpretations presented in this book are true to the best of the author's recollection. However, readers should be aware that memories can be subjective and may be influenced by the passage of time, personal bias, and the author's unique viewpoint.

Names and Identities

To protect the privacy of individuals involved, some names, identifying details, and characteristics may have been changed, fictionalized, or omitted. Any resemblance to real persons, living or dead, is purely coincidental and unintended unless explicitly stated by the author.

THE BLACKEST BLUE

Cultural and Historical Context

This book reflects the cultural and historical context in which the author lived. It includes language, attitudes, and beliefs that may be representative of the time and place described. Readers should consider historical context when interpreting the content.

Emotional and Sensitive Content

The narrative includes discussions of sensitive topics and events that may be emotionally challenging or distressing to some readers. These elements are included to provide an authentic representation of the author's experiences and are not intended to offend or harm. Reader discretion is advised.

Accuracy and Completeness

While the author has made every effort to ensure the accuracy of the information shared, there may be inadvertent errors or omissions. The book is not intended as a comprehensive or authoritative account of all events and should not be used as a sole source of factual information.

THE BLACKEST BLUE

Foreword

*T*his book follows the true story of an African American female officer in law enforcement, sharing both the good and tough moments with prisoners and the system. It tackles issues like racism, corruption, and abuse of power within her own community. As she faces these challenges, the officer makes life-changing decisions, showing resilience and determination. The narrative is a straightforward exploration of her struggle and triumph over biases in the criminal justice system, offering readers an emotionally charged perspective on the complexities she navigates.

Larry V. Starke Jr.

Life Coach • Anger Management Specialist • MEN(tor)

Dedication

Thisbook is dedicated to the love of my life, my amazing husband Mr. F. Epps, who inspired me to write. Thank you for showing me what unconditional love is, what a husband looks like, what support feels like and sounds like authentically. So many people were wrong about you. God got it right! To my awesome children, Jay R. and J.R., I love you beyond the moon and more than words can ever express. Thank you both so much for having my back, being patient with me year after year while I worked long hours, overnight, most holidays and every other weekend. See! Now I have something else to show for it. To my bonus children, I love you guys, thank you for accepting me in your life and in your heart...Z.E., F.E, Z.E, G.E., M.E. and F.E x's 2. I pray that my drive inspires you. To my loving and amazing parents, D. & L. W. for their unconditional love, countless words of encouragement and support to their children as well as so many other children and couples of all ages & ethnicities, your love is contagious. Rest well Daddy…the "page turner" as you called it… is complete! I already wrote two children's books and started on the sequel to this book.! To my loving grandmother K.H. you loved me before you knew that I would become ME...thank you Nana! For my brothers J.W., A.W., J.J. & D.W. thank you for the love, the respect and for showing up for me. To my sister NJB...you will forever have my heart, but you know that already. To GJB...You never gave up, I love you, thank you. To my Aunties aka my Funties...S.D., A.G., L.H., A.H., J.T., L.G. & J.L. it's always a good time...My Uncles, P.L., D.G, L.G. & D.T. Thank you all for loving my craziness! For my nieces... A.D., J.W., A.W., M.L. E.W., G.W. & M.W with love and affection, you are adored. To my cousins...too many to count...but whether you're an H or a W...I LOVE YOU!

To my Brooklyn family, you are solid as a rock, never wavering, never unsure about your love for me. You guys raised me on street smarts, book smarts and common sense. We learned a lot in that concrete jungle, and I wouldn't change it for the world. We stayed quick with the slick shit and questioned everything! Brownsville, never ran, never will! To my Texas family & friends, as much as I love this place, Brooklyn will always be home...lol. Thank you for making me feel safe, loved and welcomed in so many places, authentically. To my Queens family, thank you for welcoming me with open arms, my early adult life experiences were completely different because of you, thank you. For my in-laws in Pensacola Florida, especially my mother-in-law C.E., you have loved me from day 1, thank you… times a million! My dearest friends, my girls... K.S, D.C, S.J., MDH, TPG, T.M., S.L, J.J, N.F, G.H, JCM, T.H., AWW, S.W., N.P., K.M., S.P., L.B., & A.H.... Thank you for years of being there for me and remaining completely authentic with me. The shoulder, accompanied with the advice and listening to me, as I would bitch and complain and add humor…about life and work, sometimes over the phone, but usually over drinks and good food, you will always be appreciated...thank you Sis!! My OES Sistars and Masonic Brothers, battle buddies from Ft. McClellan Alabama, Suwon Korea, Giebelstadt, Kitzingen & Wuerzburg, Germany...we had some amazing times, thank you for being right there with me. I could not have done that without you. My Sarah J. Family…I love you long time…lol. For my Facebook & IG Family & Friends, don't think that I forgot about you…I could nevah! You love me from so many miles away and that love is appreciated…thank you. For my friends that allowed me to use their names…thank you. More names to come in the next 2 books. To A.S....if it wasn't for you....THANK YOU for yearssss of being there for us.

THE BLACKEST BLUE

To Nisha Yolanda and Larry V. Starke Jr. thank you for your time and attention to making sure that this baby was done right…you are appreciated more than words can express.

(If you don't see your initials…. I got you on the next one, maybe) lol

Lastly, to my thin blue line co-workers over the last 25 years, thank you to those that had my back in so many situations. I had yours too! This book is for the black and brown officers that can relate and know how hard it is to be black and blue! To my many friends of a different hue, thank you for never mistreating me, I love you too. My old colleagues from the Department of Juvenile Justice in Queens NY, my Mountain View Family, my Williamson County Family and my Travis County Family…the ones that *really* know me, one thing for sure and two things for certain….
I NEVER CHANGED…FROM DAY 1!

In closing, to anyone who has ever heard me tell a story and said, "Girl, you should write a book, I'll buy it! "

I did!! So, buy it and read it, by the way…this is the first of many.

With love,

Mrs. S. D. Epps (Author)

Synopsis

Relocating from Brooklyn to Texas, was a huge difference between how things work from the north to the south in every way. Working in the prison system, she found out that being blue pays the bills but being black and blue at the same time is the hardest thing ever. In this male dominating field, she worked in Juvenile Detention in NYC, Women's Death Row at the Mountain View Unit in Gatesville Texas, the Williamson County Sheriff's Office and lastly at the Travis County Sheriff's Office where she ultimately retired. She got to see that the more things changed, the more they stayed the same. Working in these environments where some of the most bizarre things could happen, literally from one minute to the next. It would be enough to break you if you're not strong. But if there's one thing you can count on, it's the fact that some women are calculating and heinous, while most men are spontaneous and brutal. Whether they are serving 30 years, 80 years or given the death penalty, no one can be trusted, sometimes not even your coworkers. Some of them end up trading in their work uniforms for prison uniforms, especially when they began to commit crimes themselves. No secret was safe, hell, she wasn't safe. She had to always watch her back. Turning back to the front cover of this book is an exact depiction of 25 years in law enforcement as she watched people put up a brick wall to stop her success, progress and growth. Obstacles were always in her way of being seen as equal. She watched the thin blue line, get lighter and lighter…at times the line would unravel and reveal the dark and malicious truth of hate, racism, ignorance, and defiance. Respect wasn't earned, for a black woman in uniform, especially in the sweet tea sippin' south…it was demanded and then forced! To move up to the rank of Sergeant and then to Lieutenant, she had to close her eyes to the chaos in the world happening all around her. Police brutality was and still is at an all-time high. But discussing those cases at work was at an all-time low.

Don't even think about talking about them or having an opinion…imagine 25 years of that! THEY can, but SHE better not! Not even the issues right in front of her face. They wanted her to say nothing and turn her head to blatant discrimination, abuse of power and mistreatment. For decades, politics and religion were the two things that were never discussed in a work environment, but a few years ago, it was pretty evident that all of that changed, and she was openly outnumbered. To survive in her position, she had to play the game. But she would NEVER forget who she is and where she came from! She was definitely not a yes woman and playing nice was for suckers. Crossing lines, violating policies, human and civil rights and doing it until you're numb to it, was happening as often as there was a box of donuts around…daily. Promotions withheld, opportunities hidden, positions unavailable and what exactly could she do about it? Everything! Be true to herself!! Keep her fist held up! Fight back! Make noise, say something! Do something! Don't come to work to make friends, come to make your coins and walk away with your dignity and your legacy! When the lawsuit came, the first offer of hush money was $10,000 and then $15,000… it didn't take long to realize what it would mean if she took a dime. They would want her to sign a non-disclosure agreement, and she would NEVER do that! She caught on to their bullshit and said, "No Deal"! They didn't have enough money to buy her silence! Declining that chump change allowed her the freedom of speech that she is entitled to…and that made her The Blackest Blue!

Table of Contents

THE BLACKEST BLUE

THE BLACKEST BLUE

Chapter 1

No Plan, Was Not the Plan!

By policy, I should have been promoted 19 days ago. But ever since the Sheriff lost his re-election, I haven't even been an afterthought, and for damn sure not a priority! I found myself silently thinking…

"He's probably so deep in his feelings about losing the re-election that he don't give two shits about me!"

And my black ass was probably right! I also knew the policy, but they did too. Once a person retires or resigns, the next eligible person on the list to promote is promoted immediately. Like literally the next fucking day! There's no question, no person you need to check with, that's the process. Period. I said to myself …

"Self, today! No more accepting bullshit excuses ".

I went to my desk and drafted the email. Addressing it to EVERYBODY...from my Lieutenant, all the way up to the Sheriff himself! I wanted answers, my daddy was sick, and time was of the essence! I felt bad for the Sheriff, I liked him…but he was going to have to pop the balloons to his pity party and put his tears in his pocket. I wanted...no, damn that... I demand that they promote me! I also wanted to know why they hadn't promoted me yet?? I made sure to question the timeline in writing because I was fully aware that I was getting screwed over. The sad part is, as hard as I worked to get where I was, eighteen days before a ballot had even entered into the box, they knew that they had already decided my fate. Whether he lost that re-election or not. They would rather promote a Klown...over a black woman, more specifically, THIS black woman!

When Lieutenant Louis surprised everyone with her abrupt retirement on October 29th, my promotion was supposed to take place on October 30th. But the 30th came and went. Silently.

THE BLACKEST BLUE

For days, I smiled and "played nice" as people who genuinely cared, were in the same pot of soup as the ones that were full of shit or just being nosey.

"When are they going to promote you, Sarge?"

Was starting to sound more like a taunting broken record than a sincere question. With my best asset, my beautiful smile, I would respond as upbeat as I could and say,

"Hopefully soon!"

To be honest, with the election being a week after Lt. Louis' retirement, it was literally apples and oranges, and I was being more than considerate. Being nice is a rip off!

I knew exactly what was happening, it's not like I was being impatient, because technically it wasn't just 18 days. Really, it was 305 days!! I should have been first to promote last year! I knew it and they knew that I knew it! *Countless* months of lies intertwined with 12 years of cover ups, pretending mixed with what's good for the goose just doesn't sit well with the gander bullshit. I was in the "role" of a Lieutenant, overseeing multiple departments for a year, without the official promotion or receiving the pay for the rank. I knew not to outwardly show them I was pissed off. But I was! I had every right to be, shit!

19

I didn't even bat my fake eyelashes when I came in second on the promotion list. Mainly because everyone knew the truth.

Even the idiot that came in 1st place was shocked that he beat me.

Officers from every department, white, black, hispanic, old timers and new hires...would stop me in the hallway and say, "YOU came in second??? No fucking way!!!" I played it off like he won fair and square, but I wanted to question how it was even *legally* possible for me to lose? I mean with the winner being under an internal affairs investigation THE DAY we took the written test was...wait, I'm getting ahead of myself here.

This whole situation felt familiar, I've seen this and experienced this before. It reminded me of the way people feel when they get back together with an ex. The minute they start doing the same old shit as before, showing those same patterns, you're like *"Ooohhhhh yeah, that's why it didn't work out the first time! Got it!"*

I started to look up the word –insanity- in the dictionary and see if there was a picture of me next to the word with my tongue sticking out like these new female rappers. But that would have just been another waste of my time.

THE BLACKEST BLUE

Before the promotions, the accusations, before the false claims of me creating a hostile work environment. Before the secret petition to get rid of me, which I later found out about. Before I ever felt like I was being discriminated against, I had my heart broken by my *own*. Yeah, now that, boy I tell you, that's a different kind of pain. That shit will hit you and hurt you differently. I had already worked for the Department of Juvenile Justice in New York for over three years when I decided to relocate to Texas. Being an Army veteran, I knew to look up my Eastern Star sisters and some of my old battle buddies in order to get around this new town.

After a few weeks of unpacking, organizing, settling in and boredom, I went out to eat with these sisters I met back when I was stationed in Germany.

We met up at a diner that everyone claims has the best fried fish plates in town, hands down.

"The fried catfish is delish!" Gwen said.

Before I could agree or disagree, Lucy immediately followed up in a whispered voice,

"So, are you working yet?"

I could tell by the look on Gwen's face, that Lucy must have already asked her that same question about me in the car.

"No, not yet...but it's time to start looking, my lil savings is drying up."

I joked, to ease the knife cutting through the tense air. Lucy giggled with me, but Gwen didn't find my joke funny at all and ended my comedy act with the quickness.

"Girl, ain't shit funny with a 4-year-old at the house. What did you do before you moved here?"

Gwen asked. I straightened up, like I was talking to a drill sergeant.

Gwen was dead serious, but she was right, being unemployed and not having my own place, with a 4-year-old as a single parent, wasn't funny to anybody.

I moved to Texas at the end of January, and we were in this diner having this conversation over fried catfish in the middle of April. When I left Brooklyn, I didn't have a plan A...B or C. I just left. Quit my full time and my part-time job for the cost-of-living Texas had to offer me. I had a little over six thousand dollars in the bank when my flight landed in January 2004. Four months unemployed and it doesn't take a math whiz to realize, all withdrawals plus no deposits will quickly equal to...broke as fuck!

I was pinching from my savings little by little and I do mean pinching. I couldn't tell you what the hell I was thinking back then by relocating with no job lined up, but I was winging it.

Looking back, that was foolish and irresponsible, but I did just that. I can tell you what I'm thinking right now though,

"Don't try that shit at home!"

Once I told Gwen about working in NYC for a little over three years with the Department of Juvenile Justice, her face lit up. She said,

"Shitttt, girlllll that's right up my alley! I can tell you what to do to get a job at the prison. You ready to go back to work??

"Hell yeah, I'm ready!" I said with a mouthful of fried catfish.

"I got you Sis!" Gwen said sternly.

Gwen was a woman of her word, because she did exactly that. I mean a fool proof, step-by-step, don't fuck this up, list of dos and don'ts to follow, on getting a job as a Corrections Officer. Well, she left out one very important piece of instruction.

THE BLACKEST BLUE

She didn't tell me what to wear to the interview. I'm a New Yorker, I showed up to the Texas Workforce Commission for my corrections exam in a two-piece pants suit with a 3-quarter length jacket and high heeled boots. Not a hair out of place and my make-up was flawless. Yep, sticking right out like a sore thumb as I sat in a room near 9 other people, in jeans, sneakers and t-shirts. Raise your hand if you're overdressed! SMH.

That was my first taste of too extra reality pie. This is nothing like NYC! For one... the exam was FREE! That would never happen for a State or City exam, ever.

I was also expecting the line for the candidates to be down the block and around the corner. When the state representative administering the test entered the classroom and closed the door, I couldn't believe that was it...all ten of us were testing for the job.

Compared to the fifteen hundred that would have showed up if we were in New York City, this was unreal. We were previously informed to bring our driver's licenses, birth certificates, social security cards and high school diplomas, if we moved on in the process. I'm literally four months out of Brooklyn so as soon as the test was done, I figured we'd go home and stalk the mailbox for at least 6 months to a year, waiting for the snail mail results.

Wrong again. The examiner said he was going to grade the tests right away and we could take a 15-minute break before returning to the classroom.

I'm starting to like it here in Texas, I thought. We all went into the hallway, a few headed in the restrooms, as expected. You could hear people asking each other,

"What answer did you put for #3?"

I just stood off to the side alone. Observing how things worked out here in this red state.

After a few minutes, I noticed the examiner slowly walking down the hallway. Looking down at the ID cards in his hands, it was evident that he was trying to match the face on the IDs with people in the hallway. I watched two guys get a slight shoulder tap, enter the classroom, grab their belongings and vacate the premises.

Within minutes of their exit, we were all summoned back into the classroom and informed that we had all passed the exam...and then there were eight!

We were told that our official letter with the prison assignment would eventually arrive in the mail and to just keep an eye out for it.

THE BLACKEST BLUE

After a few more days of reorganizing, boredom and mailbox stalking, I decided to stop by Lowe's for a few things.

I was about 4 cars away from the handicap parking, or as we refer to them, the military VIP parking spaces, when I saw a woman driving like a bat out of hell, coming in from the wrong angle in a big body Benz. Screech parking as we made eye contact, she jumped out of her car and ran in the door while simultaneously throwing on a red employee vest. All I can see from the back was, pants that were too tight to be professional and long booty length blonde weave.

Chapter 2

Tamika and the Big Body Benz

I know this chick saw me!! I banged on my steering wheel. I even had my left blinker on. I said out loud to no one.

"Oh, she definitely want to get cursed out!"

Truth be told, I was still too Brooklyn at this point. So, you already know I'm going to find her ass and tell her about herself, but I have some retail therapy and some calming down to handle first. I could go from 0 to 100 real quick. So let me shop and woosah, I thought. As I'm browsing, I hear,

"Ma'am, can I help you find anything?"

I politely declined, because as nice as this employee appeared to be, I was still looking for the parking spot thief. I was going to tell her a thing or two...or even three!

As I headed towards the home décor section, guess who was hard at work...yep, you guessed it. The booty length blonde weave, parking spot bandit with the too tight pants and the big body Benz. I watched her nervously strike up a conversation with a customer. We made eye contact, for the second time today and I could tell that she knew it was me. Or maybe she picked up on the death glare that I was burning her drawn on eyebrows off with.

Who knows, she may have even felt self-conscious because of the weave track that was showing when she bent down, but either way, she was uncomfortable. Good, I thought!

As the other customer was walking away, she didn't even let the opportunity for me to embarrass her or myself take place. I looked at the white paper used for the name tag in her red vest. "Tamika", I will never forget her name, I thought. She wasted no time and nervously said,

"I'm sorry, I know that was you that I cut off, but I couldn't afford to be late one more time and I hope you can forgive me? Please don't be mad at me, look, I'll even mark all your stuff 75% off but that's the most I can do."

I cracked up laughing and said,

" No, you don't have to do all of that, as good as that discount sounds, I just applied to get a prison job, not cause you to lose your job! But I forgive you and thank you for apologizing. I'm always late to everything, so I completely understand."

Tamika continued helping me and the more we talked the more I was glad that I kept my composure, she ended up being cool as hell. Cool enough to let me fix that weave track that was showing, and we both laughed our asses off. She told me that they were hiring, and she had connections with the manager on duty. All I had to do was say the word and she would go talk to him, plus she felt like she still owed me one, since I declined the discount. Now trust me, I wanted that discount, but I don't trust that people just do shit for you, out of the kindness of their heart…you always end up owing them something in return. I was going to think about it, but I thought about my daughter and the look that Gwen had on her face at the restaurant and decided to cash in on that!

"Ok, now I'll take you up on THAT offer, but don't forget what I told you, I just applied for a job at the prison, I don't want Lowe's to think I'll be around for long, temporary or part-time will do".

Excited to prove to me that she had the kind of pull she told me that she had, and to make up for this morning's parking space heist, she ran off and left me in aisle 11 all alone. Tamika was also a woman of her word. In less than ten minutes, she was taking me to the back where a mob of red vests were eating out of Tupperware bowls and talking shit about the previous night's game. I applied online, the manager made some calls to Human Resources while I waited, and for once, not cleaning out my car came in handy.

I still had my personal documents with me and a little pep in my step as I went to go get them. Tamika walked me outside to get my envelope and the minute we both noticed how crooked she parked; we cracked up laughing again.

The process was smooth and faster than expected, but let me be the one to tell you, my first day was damn near my last day!

I kid you not. That manual labor for the pay offered was not for ya' girl. Coming from New York, making more than double of what they offered here, without any strenuous work, this job is **definitely** on the list of underpaid jobs. I put my pride aside and got through it for my kid but also for my bank account. A little something was better than a lot of nothing. I was honestly grateful for Tamika.

THE BLACKEST BLUE

Hitting it off with her also worked in my favor because she came in on her day off to train me in the same department she worked in, Home Decor. Unbeknownst to me, that was the deal she made with the manager. God, Jehovah, Budda, and The Virgin Mary must have heard my prayers because after leaving work on my first day exhausted, I checked the mailbox and realized that my stalking spree was over, there it was!

I pulled out the overstuffed envelope and began to read.

"From the Texas Department of Criminal Justice.

Dear Sir/Ma'am

Congratulations! You are receiving this letter as a conditional offer of employment with the Texas Department of Criminal Justice. We have completed your background check and if you are still interested in working with us, please give us a call at blah, blah, blah.

Your corrections academy start date is:

June 10, 2004. After you have successfully completed all tests and physical requirements, blah, blah, blah. You will be required to pass a defensive tactics course, qualify on a 15-gauge shotgun, an AR-15, a pistol and you'll also be pepper sprayed. You will be expected to complete blah, blah

31

blah. Upon graduation, you will be permanently assigned to the:

Mountain View Unit in Gatesville, Texas."

I couldn't call Gwen fast enough to tell her that I was on my way to her house. She could tell by my tone that I was excited and had some good news to share. As she opened the door, I had a big smile on my face, and I held the envelope up like it was a winning lottery ticket. Gwen was warm and loving like a big sister. I knew that her tough love was harmless, she just wanted what was best for me. I watched her remove the packet of papers from the envelope and flip straight to the last page. She had been working as a corrections officer for 10 years at this point. Recommending people over and over meant that she knew the drill.

She knew that what she was looking for would be on the last page. As her eyes met with the words on the paper, shockingly she said,

"Oh, shit girl!"

Panicked I said, *"What's wrong?"* Gwen said, *"Bitch, they got you going to work at the Death Row unit for women!"*

If a black person could turn as white as a ghost, go ahead and enter my name as Coco Casper in the Guinness Book of

THE BLACKEST BLUE

World Records. I was in shock and immediately, all I could think about was "The Green Mile" and "Ol' Sparky".

I called my mom in New York and told her what working at The Mountain View Unit in Gatesville Texas really meant.

"Whoa! Death Row as in executions?" she asked.

I just shrugged my shoulders but didn't say a word over the phone. Simply because I didn't know the answer, and the shock had not worn off yet.

"Well, mommy continued, they probably took into consideration that you have experience from working with Juveniles here and your 5 years of active-duty service in the Army. Look on the bright side, that will be an impressive entry on your resume.'"

Boy was she right, as usual. My second day on the job, I showed up with my two weeks' notice and my overstuffed envelope in my hand. I was excited to show Tamika what happened when I checked the mail last night. I also needed to ask her who I should give my notice to, but I didn't see her in Home Decor. I went to appliances, flooring and the paint department, no Tamika.

Chapter 3
Surprise, Surprise!

I knew she was on the schedule for today. I double checked it. I even tried the lady's restroom. Nothing. I didn't know anyone to ask but the one guy that was in orientation with me and he worked nights. Maybe she was running late, again, damn I hope they don't fire her ass. I thought,

"Awww man, we didn't even exchange phone numbers because everything went so quickly, I'll make sure to ask her for it today when she gets here."

THE BLACKEST BLUE

I clocked in and the day got super busy, really fast. They had me float from different departments and turn off the call buttons.

As I lied to the waiting customers by telling them, *"Someone will be with you shortly."*

Every chance I got to go in the back or to walk a customer to another department, I did.

Maybe she called in sick or maybe they gave her the day off since she came in yesterday on her day off to train me, I continued to speculate. Around noon, it was finally time for my break, I had my food in Tupperware just like everyone else. Shittt, learned my lesson with that two-piece pants suit, I didn't want to be too extra, again. If I don't talk, they won't know that I'm not from here, so I'll just eat and quietly keep to myself. But as soon as I entered the break room, the red vests were engrossed in some juicy gossip and you know black people, we do theatrical re-enactments, voice overs and earn Oscar awards when we tell a story! They never even noticed when I came in and sat down.

"How much!!??"

The older black man asked in a raised voice. According to the name on the white paper in the pocket of his red vest, his name was Edward. The younger red vest said,

THE BLACKEST BLUE

"Four thousand dollars!!!".

They all gasped in unison as if they had rehearsed it. Edward grabbed his shirt and pretended to clutch his heart as he did his best impression of Fred Sanford.

"Damn!! FOUR GRAND?? How did they catch it?"

he asked, as the younger red vest held everyone captive with her detailed description of events. I too was being held in captivity.

I spent all morning looking for Tamika only to find out she wasn't late or sick, her ass was in the county jail!

Apparently, after I left yesterday, she helped a customer walk out to their truck with enough lumber to build a privacy fence around their entire property and their neighbors too! She walked by the registers and did not pass GO or collect $200.00. The cashier was in on it too, so they were both arrested on the spot, courtesy of the Loss Prevention team. Of course, the jokes started immediately, and they all took a turn throwing jabs at the situation. Imitating her trying to look normal walking with a shopping cart full of empty boxes stacked on top of their Tupperware containers to simulate a large quantity. The visual she gave made it seem like it was so much lumber that a blind man would have caught them in the act.

THE BLACKEST BLUE

"Damn, was she trying to build a clubhouse?"

A red vest asked. Followed by…

"How in the hell did she get fired on her day off?"

They all erupted in laughter and started to trickle out of the breakroom shaking their heads as they returned to their individual departments and back to normal.

The rest of the day was a blur, and I was working in a fog. Tamika seemed so nice, but I guess if she was willing to give me everything for 75% off, two minutes after meeting me, you really can't put anything past anybody. That big body Benz had to get paid for somehow and logically there was no way she paid the car note for a Benz on $7.75 an hour.

I found a manager to give my two-week resignation notice to, and honestly, I was glad that I wouldn't be there much longer now that Tamika was gone. I also didn't want to be labeled "guilty by association". The next 13 days felt just like it did when my mother would ask for my report card every day after school, a dread. I made sure that I had everything on my recommended packing list for training. I didn't want to need anything or come up short when June 10th came. I never heard an update or even knew Tamika's last name to inquire about her. I shrugged that entire encounter off and kept moving forward. The first week of the academy was mostly paperwork, boring state mandated videos and on Wednesday, 2 SURPRISE TESTS...one pop quiz and one drug test. Now why would anyone apply for the prison and still get high? That was the million-dollar question... but they do it!

Same routine as before, take a break and they'll call everyone back in when they're done checking both test results. Same as before, but this time four people got the shoulder tap. However, they were not allowed to just get their things and go. This time, they had to be escorted off state property and informed to never apply again. We all got our passing grades, high fived, repositioned the classroom to fill in for the four vacant desks and gossiped about the ones that failed the drug test after training, near our cars in the parking lot.

Sergeant Tommy Gonzalez was a well-respected and well-loved instructor. He told us that we were about to do an early morning road march all around the prison grounds. I raised my hand and asked,

"Sarge, do you allow cadets to call the cadence?"

"Only if they know what they're doing, but ok Brooklyn, I'll give you a shot". He said sarcastically.

THE BLACKEST BLUE

I remembered a lot of cadences from my time in the Army, but there was one in particular that would work here, just like it did in basic training. We started out marching in a military style formation. As soon as we turned down the street, there was nothing in our way but fields, cows and convicted felons.

Sergeant Gonzalez said. *" Ok Brooklyn don't let me down."*

It was showtime, and dammit it was go time!

" Ok cadets, every time I say, "You left", all together respond loud and thunderous with "You're right!"

I repeated the instructions and did a quiet practice sample for them to pick up the rhythm.

They were excited, pumped up and ready to hear the whole thing out loud!

"Your momma was there when you left"

"You're Right!!"

"Your daddy was there when you left"

"You're Right!!"

"Your cat, your dog, your fish, your frog...was in your home when you left"

THE BLACKEST BLUE

"You're Right!!"

"Your car was there when you left"

"You're Right!!"

Your friends were there when you left"

"You're Right!!"

Your keys, your phone, your honey, your money, was in your home when you left"

"You're Right!!"

Sound off... 1-2 Sound off..3-4

Sound off..1-2...3-4!!

When I looked back for the approval of how I was doing, Sergeant Gonzalez was holding his stomach laughing and the other instructors were cracking up too. They were all giving me the thumbs up, fueling me to keep on going with the cadence. I added more loved ones and material possessions left behind for the prisoners to think about as they stopped plowing the fields and listened in closely. I was making it up as I went along, and they were loving every second. We did it Brooklyn! I thought. Biggie would have been proud. Shit anybody from my old neighborhood would have been so proud of me in that moment. Brooklyn is the definition of that old Frank Sinatra line in the song New York, New York. *"If I can make it there, I'll make it anywhere!"* When we returned to the classroom, everyone was hyped up talking about the cadence.

" I just heard my favorite cadence ever! I never had a cadet do that one before, so be ready every morning when we go out to do it, Great job Brooklyn!" Sergeant Gonzalez beamed.

I said, *"Yes Sir! I'll be ready and thank you for giving me a shot!"* Smiling, proud and excited …because of his stamp of approval, people stopped asking me to say silly shit like *"Coffee and water"* every damn day, just to hear my Brooklyn accent. These farmers as I refer to Texans, started respecting me more and more as they could see, whatever stereotype they had in their heads about New Yorkers, was on a totally different perspective now. All of us are not rude and in a hurry all the damn time. Sarcastic…yes, loud…hell yes… but not always rude.

It was our first weekend off in what would be a ten-week training academy. Bright and early Saturday morning, my daughter and I were boarding a plane for Norfolk Virginia. Killing two birds with one stone, my goal was to meet up with my parents at our family reunion and let them take my baby girl back to NYC, while I continued in the corrections academy. I didn't request permission to go out of town because this was only a turnaround trip. The plan was for us to dip out early Saturday and return alone Sunday morning. Suitcase for her, bookbag for me, in and out, easy peasy. I would be back in time for barracks clean up and room inspections Sunday evening, with my trip undetected. More importantly, I would be ready for formation bright and early Monday morning, at least that's what was SUPPOSED to happen!

Chapter 4

TSA or KKK???

*T*he family reunion was just what I needed, the home cooked food was amazing, the DJ was on point, and it was nice to see some familiar faces. I had been in Texas for six months by then, so yeah, I needed that dose of family love.

My parents were on a cloud, their one and only grandchild was back in their arms, and I was so glad that I was able to spend time with them too. Most of my cousins I hadn't seen in years and others I got to meet for the first time. One thing for sure, we were definitely related! We were all spontaneous, wild, comical and crazy!

THE BLACKEST BLUE

Early Sunday morning, my parents drove me back to Norfolk airport, I gave them, and my baby girl hugs and kisses and on I went, headed back to Texas, or so I thought.

As I go through the TSA security check, I heard a beep coming from the metal detector. An older Caucasian lady waves me over with the hand wand and immediately starts checking for weapons of mass destruction at the top of my head. No bobby pins, no weave, no beep. As she scans my stomach, the beep was louder and I giggled as I said,

"Oh, Ma'am, I just got a belly piercing yesterday, all of my cousins at the fam-"

She cut me off mid-sentence and, in her bible-belt, southern accent, she sternly let me know

"I don't care what you and your cousins did honey, you wanna get on that there flight, I suggest you go and take that thang out!"

In utter disbelief and shock, I said, *"I can show it to you, it's not a weapon or anything crazy like that!"*

As the agent is shaking her full head of gray hair from side to side to indicate that she wasn't interested, I asked,

"Well, what's the black curtain in the corner right there for?

THE BLACKEST BLUE

As I pointed to what was obviously a privacy curtain. I was certain that it was for a situation such as this. This middle-aged white woman looked at that curtain and looked back at me like that curtain was a figment of my imagination.

Her facial expression said, *"What curtain?"* I knew then that I was up Shit's Creek without a paddle.

Not one of the TSA employees pretended to be of any assistance, at all.

They also didn't attempt to hide their hatred. Apparently *"none"* of them saw the black curtain.

"You either go in the bathroom and take that "thang" out or you're not catching that flight!"

Heavy emphasis on *"that thang"* for the second time and by the scowl on her face, that was not a threat. She meant that shit!

I said, *"There must be someone I can reason with, please... can I speak to your supervisor?"*

After I asked for the supervisor, I instantly regretted it.

As soon as the TSA supervisor walked over, it was like I had summonsed the wife of the Grand Wizard of the KKK!

Jesus Christ! The look on her face was of pure evil stirred with disgust.

The other TSA workers had shit eating grins on their faces. Silently letting me know that I had gone from bad to worse with my request. The fact that she had to sit her cup of coffee down to address the likes of me, pissed her off. As I attempted to explain that I had just gotten the belly piercing yesterday and that it would be painful to remove or that it could get infected, Agnes, according to her name tag, said in a snuff spittin' Moonshine drinking, drawl straight out of an old Western movie.

"Look ah' here darlin', September 11th changed errthang round' here, so you either take it out or take the bus!"

The only thing she didn't say was "Now nigger!"

I literally could not win this battle. I didn't mention the black curtain or any other options, that made logical sense to me, because she made it very clear that there were **zero** options. I went in the nearest bathroom and tried to ease the piercing out, but it was way too tender. I couldn't take the pain, and time was literally running out. There were no other flights to Austin that would get me back tonight. It was either this flight or I would be a no-show at the academy tomorrow morning.

I had no choice, and every last one of those racist bitches knew that!

I ripped the piercing away from my brown skin and used a wad of tissue to pat the trickle of blood from gliding down my abdomen and another wad of tissue to pat the tear that escaped my eyeball for so many different reasons.

I walked through the metal detector, with my head held high and anticipated the silence. I had already thrown the belly piercing away and swore to never replace it. With no beeping sound to deal with, I kept on walking forward. I didn't even need to look back to see them have an orgasm over their minor victory. Fuck them, I had a flight to catch!

Chapter 5

New Job, New Home, New Me

I stayed quiet for a few days, reflecting on my encounter with the TSA agents at Norfolk airport. It's not like I could have shared that experience or even told anyone about the incident because my black ass didn't tell anyone that I was going out of town! Now, I definitely told my parents, but not one soul at the training academy. I didn't trust any of those farmers just yet. So, I pretended everything was fine. Just as fate would have it, after three days of rain, the sun was out, and it was time for a road march. Thank God! Sergeant G. gave me a head nod, and I knew what time it was! I was looking forward to getting out of that funk too. Showtime, go time!

THE BLACKEST BLUE

I had to focus my attention on something positive. Over the last few weeks, I had been looking for my own space to live in, checking out listings for affordable places every chance I got. My old battle buddy Foisset was letting me house sit while she and her fiancé were deployed in Iraq. Another win/win situation.

What a blessing that was. It honestly worked out for both of us. However, Foisset was on her way back for good in less than a month and the clock was ticking. My parents blessed me with a car, so I didn't have a note to worry about or daycare for right now, Thank God. The way that our schedule worked while we were in training was… Monday through Friday, we had the option to drive up to the academy from wherever you lived. Some cadets lived in Waco, others lived in Temple, but the option was 45 minutes to an hour in one direction.

Or you had the option to stay in the barracks during the week and drive 2 minutes away to the next parking lot at the training academy where the classroom was located.

That was a no-brainer. I got a room in the barracks as soon as I got back from Virginia. On Fridays after class, they gave us the option to go home for the weekend or stay there, which I never ever did. I would leave every Friday, go to Foisset's place, do laundry, relax and study. That next Saturday morning, I got up and went to the first place on my list. I remembered the ad said,

"Black owned", "Veteran owned and operated real estate agency".

After the customer service I received in Virginia, I needed to feel safe. I walked up to the door and through the window, I saw a very tall, older black man with a Jheri curl.

He was well dressed and even wore suspenders. I giggled at how dated he looked as opposed to how older men dressed in NYC. I think the last time I saw suspenders; I was a kid I remember my little brother Jabari had some on when we went to church years ago. I told the gentleman what kind of place I was looking for and what my dilemma was with getting paid only once a month. From what I could tell, he was a kind soul and an understanding gentle giant. I swear he was almost 7 feet tall. I wanted to ask him if he ever played basketball professionally but I'm certain that he has been asked that question a zillion times in his lifetime. So, I opted to not even bother. He listened with his heart and said he would work with me. Look at God!

Mr. Senegal said, *"I'll tell you what, I have quite a few you might like, but I have a 3-bedroom, with 2 bathrooms, 2 living rooms and a 2-car garage residential home for*

$795.00 a month that you'll love! You just need your own washer and dryer, but it's in a good neighborhood, you give me the full amount for rent and half of the deposit this month and the other half of the deposit with your rent next month, you have a deal."

"*$795.00??!!?* I asked in a high-pitched voice.

"*That's it, just $795.00!!??*" I asked again.

He laughed and said,

"*You want me to charge you more?*"

"*No, Sir! Please forgive me, I moved here from Brooklyn a few months ago. I'm just shocked at the cost of living here, I'm used to paying more for way less, but yes, I would love to see them, if that's ok with you?*"

Mr. Senegal, said that was no problem, all he needed was my driver's license and he would give me the address and the key to go and look at it. I could not believe this southern hospitality. Giving me the key and allowing me to go alone without an employee from his office damn near made me go into shock! He said the most he could give me was 3 keys to 3 different properties and I thought, "What kind of trust and honor system they got going on in Texas? Not only would this never happen in New York, but this gave me hope for what Texas had to offer in my future. I went to the first address he gave me, the one he thought I would like the most and he was right. It was a beautiful home, manicured lawn, hedges shaped like oranges, clean inside and out and a large backyard...bigger than any yard I'd seen in Brooklyn or Queens combined. It was on a nice side of town too.

Bigger than what I needed, but it was affordable plus it was safe, and in a few minutes, it would be mine! After locking up tight, I ran to the bank and got the money orders before he could change his mind. I didn't even want to see the other two. As promised, we signed the lease, and he gave me 2 sets of keys. He told me the locks would be re-keyed in an hour if I had time to wait and you know I waited!! The place was perfect for us, and I was grateful at how fast things were coming together. You know I called my mother and told her what happened.

We laughed and cried at where I started from with no plan at all, to the way things were going. She was so proud of what I had accomplished in less than a year. My dad yelled though the phone,

"Hurry up and unpack so we can come and visit!"

I promised my parents that the next day, before returning to the barracks, I would find a church to go to and thank God for these blessings. Randomly, I picked a church that wasn't too far from my new place. I am always running late but I made it to the praise and worship service at 11:00 on the dot. I sat down in the 4th pew from the altar on the left and as soon as I turned my head to slide down, there was Mr. Senegal and his wife Gi-Gi smiling and happy to see me. I just cried and cried at the coincidence because he never even mentioned his church,

"*what are the chances?* I thought to myself.

Prison tours were on the schedule for the week, and we had to have a special meeting with the Major over the corrections academy. Major Connor was the perfect balance for leadership.

He didn't make statements based off of race or economic status, he was direct and straight to the point. He informed us that we would be touring several units, to include the women's death row unit, "Mountain View" where I would be assigned and the Hughes's Unit which is an all-male unit. Where we won't be going today is the Lane Murray Unit, he said with certainty. Due to the bounty that's on the head of the woman that killed the singer Selena, it was not safe for a new officer to have contact with her or even get close enough to find out where she was being held in protective custody. As we began to load up in the vans, we could hear them making references to people from Corpus Christi applying for a job at the prison in Gatesville, hoping to oblige the bounty. A million dollars was a lot of money back in 2004.

I was willing to bet that there was enough rage from Selena's fans, that they would have taken her killer out for free! Major Connor joined us for the road march earlier that morning and you already know Sergeant G. had me out there showing off. Not only did they all love when I called the cadence, but I scored high on my exams too. I was feeling pretty good about this career choice. Those ten weeks in the academy went by pretty fast. After graduation, you got reassigned to your home unit where you would do three more weeks of, on the job training with a mentor. We were all excited to put this training behind us, all 26 of us. Graduation was bittersweet because, some of us knew we would never see each other again. We had created a bond that would immediately disappear after the ceremony. There was no Facebook or IG back then.

A few of us exchanged phone numbers and said we would stay in contact. Knowing damn well...we wont.

The day after graduation, I got a call from one of the cadets that I hung out with in class during training. Officer Rutledge asked me if I wanted to go out to "Club Night Life" with her and her sister Tisha. Excited, I agreed because after all of that training, defensive tactics and getting pepper sprayed, we needed to go out and let our hair down. Rutledge sent me a text with her address on it and asked that I park my car at her house, so that we could take a cab together. The last thing we wanted to do as new Corrections Officers was drink and drive. That's career suicide. When she answered the door, she had a look on her face that told me, something was not ok.

Chapter 6

Fake Ike vs Real Ike

A s I stepped in and greeted her sister Tisha, Rutledge's husband and his homeboy appeared from the kitchen, and he said,

"Everybody ready?"

The smirk on his face was a clear indicator that his intention was to ruin "girl's night". Rutledge and I made eye contact and communicated nonverbally. My eyes said, *"You didn't tell me your husband was coming"* and her eyes said, *"I'll tell you later"*. We pretended to be happy with our surprise chaperones, loaded up in the cab and were on our way. The body language between the husband and wife, was beyond tense.

As soon as we passed the threshold of the club, Rutledge grabbed my arm and said,

"I gotta pee". Every woman knows that's code for... *"we need to talk, now!".* The men went inside, and we beelined for the lady's room.

"Shit! Shit! What am I going to do now?

Rutledge was in a full-on panic. However, I was oblivious to the real problem, I said,

" Girl please, just enjoy yourself and the atmosphere, let's go get a drink."

Tisha, her sister started shaking her head and said,

"Nette, did you even try to stop him?"

"I couldn't, he was watching every movement I made, there was just no time." Rutledge responded.

She then turned to me and said,

"I invited my side dude to the club, not knowing my husband was going to pull this stunt."

My eyes grew wide as hell, and as I'm shaking my head… everything made sense.

"So, call him right now and tell him not to come!"

But it was too late, when we got out of the cab, she saw his truck in the parking lot.

" Holy Shit! Girl this is a mess!"

"Nowwww do you understand?". Rutledge asked.

I nodded as we exited the bathroom and made our way to the bar. We strategically placed ourselves where we could see the door and her hubby surveilling us from across the room. Instead of letting my hair down, I felt like it was in a tight librarian's bun because I was on high alert. So much for enjoying myself. As the crowd started to get heavier, it became more and more difficult for Mr. Rutledge to keep his eye on the target.

Pretty soon, some ass shaking in front of his section on the dance floor distracted the overbearing husband as he forgot all about his sneaky ass wife.

Speaking of which, she was the one getting up and going to the bar to refill our drinks each time. Not out of generosity, purely out of opportunity. Once the DJ announced a booty shaking contest, everyone in the club was focused on the half-naked contestants as they walked on stage one by one.

The chance to sneak outside was now and Rutledge didn't miss a nanosecond in the window of opportunity to escape. As she gave us the nod from the bar, we were already prepared for the lie we would tell if imitation Ike Turner noticed that Shannette was missing. As the MC of the show started to explain the rules, the crowd began to scream in anticipation as the beat dropped.

Taunting with the crowd, the DJ would start the music and then stop it.

After three times of starting and stopping that booty bounce music, he changed the energy and put on "Pony" by Ginuwine.

The base alone had the ladies on stage showing out. Before contestant #3 could turn around and bend over, imitation Ike Turner was standing in front of us like a high school principal.

"Where's Shannette?!"

Without missing a beat, me and Tisha said at the same time,

"At the bar getting our drinks."

Looking back on it now, we sounded like we rehearsed that shit, but he believed us and went straight to the bar looking for his wife.

Lucky for us, there were 4 bars in this club and since we didn't point in either direction, he set out to check each one.

Mr. Rutledge was far from a fool. He checked 2 of the bar areas and had his homeboy check the other 2.

When the men met back up, they approached us together and this time, fake Ike Turner was looking more like the real Ike Turner.

He looked directly at Tisha with fire in his eyes and demanded,

"Nette better appear here real soon or she's going to have a fucking problem tonight!"

I jumped up from my chair and said,

"Let me go check the bathroom, there's no need to trip, damn!" I didn't even know him well enough to talk to him like that, but I was pissed off! I didn't sign up for this bullshit, and instantly wished I had stayed home.

When I walked away from my seat, he sat in it to let me know he'll be waiting right there for me to return with his prized possession.

I was so concerned about what would happen if I came back empty-handed, that I knew if I didn't find her, I was going to take a cab to my car and let them sort that mess out for themselves.

Thank God the ladies' room was near the front door. Just as I was about to enter the bathroom, a fight broke out. Perfect timing! I couldn't have planned that better myself. I needed that distraction because I knew damn well Rutledge wasn't in the bathroom.

I walked directly out of the front door to the club and looked in the parking lot for a truck.

Right there in plain sight, on the back row in the parking lot, under a damn light pole, I can see Rutledge stupid ass kissing her side dude in the front seat of his truck!

I thought to myself *"This girl is crazy! If I can see her, I'm sure her husband could if he came outside to look for her!"*

Worse than being visible and carefree, this dummy didn't even lock the doors.

You can't even make this shit up! I yanked the passenger side door open and said,

"Are you fucking crazy? He's in there looking for you and he's pissed off!!" As she stepped out of the truck, I slammed

THE BLACKEST BLUE

the door and motioned for the guy to drive off and he had the audacity to look sad like he really didn't want to leave. Shannette wrapped her arms around me and just started crying.

Now I don't know if these tears are from being unhappily married or if it was because she was intoxicated. But to me, she was far more drunk now than I remembered 30 minutes ago.

I was holding her up and leading her back into the club when we saw Tisha, Mr. Rutledge and his homeboy walking towards us.

"What the fuck you doin' out here Nette?"

he asked as his eyes cased the parking lot.

"She needed some air; she was in the bathroom overheated". I lied. I could see him trying to process whether I was telling the truth or not, but he knows his wife and the level of trust in this marriage was at ground zero. We all squeezed into a cab for the second time tonight. Since she didn't feel well, Rutledge climbed in first. Mr. Rutledge was in the middle and his homeboy was next to him. Tisha and I sat in the front next to the driver.

The same seating arrangement we had when we arrived at the club. Knowing his wife better than I did, we could all hear Mr. Rutledge working himself up and getting angrier.

"Where the fuck were you?" he demanded.

A question that was not whispered and he didn't care who could hear him. The cab driver shot a concerned look in the rear-view mirror.

Tisha said, *"Bro, chill out, you see that she don't feel good".*

"Ain't shit wrong with this motherfucker, she think she slick, that's the only thing wrong with her ass. She not sick and she not drunk!"

He responded to Tisha without taking his eyes off of Shannette or even blinking for that matter.

I still don't understand why Rutledge tried to pull this stunt after knowing her husband was coming and was already suspicious of her ass.

Clearly, she wasn't getting away with faking sick and drunk. Not in his eyes anyway. He assumed she was up to no good and because he had no proof, that's all he could do...assume.

We could tell he was frustrated, and the liquor didn't help the situation out one bit. Just as he got quiet and things started to chill out... we all heard Rutledge's phone vibrate,

"Buzz, buzz, buzz, buzz". The side dude chose this precise moment to profess his love in a text that Shannette's hands were not fast enough to hide from Mr. Rutledge's eyes.

"Who the fuck is that Nette?!

"I don't know" she shrugged her shoulders. Keeping her eyes closed as she lied.

"Oh, so a random number was glad he got to see you tonight, huh bitch? How you don't know who the fuck it is but a random number text you and said, "Damn Nette you got some soft ass lips!! I knew it! I fucking knew it, wait until we get home!"

He was breathing like a bull mixed with a dragon and there was no calming him. Rutledge had fucked up and she knew it! The drunk and sick act was over with, there would be no getting out of the stunt she pulled and from the way Mr. Rutledge was behaving from the beginning of the night, it was evident that he already knew his wife was cheating on him.

I couldn't tell if the cab driver was driving slow out of fear or if he wanted to see how this was going to play out, but I needed him to hurry his ass up so I can get to my car. Before the cabbie could put the car in park, Rutledge bolted from the back door and took off running down the street, barefoot.

THE BLACKEST BLUE

Her husband was right behind her ass like a police foot pursuit. She ran to a neighbor's house that had the porch light on and banged on the door like Fred Flintstone.

As her husband got closer, she ran to the next neighbor's house like a game of dodge ball was being played. She ran through the grass to another house, but the sprinkler system slowed her pace down and he caught up to her.

There was no time to stop the rage that was built up in the mixture of hurt, betrayal and a few shots of Hennessy. As if he was defending himself against a heavy weight boxer and not his own wife, Mr. Rutledge dropped his opponent like a sack of potatoes.

Tisha screamed, *"Oh my God, Nette!! Stop hitting my sister, somebody call the cops!!"* The cab driver called the police as some of the porch lights started to illuminate from the late-night chaos happening on Rockaway Avenue.

Chapter 7

Decisions, Decisions

"Come on Bro!"

Yelled the homeboy as he left the passenger door wide open to the getaway car. Mr. Rutledge didn't stay around to see if he caused major damage or broke any bones. He left his lying ass wife badly beaten in a pile of avoidable hurt and pain. This didn't seem outlandish to anyone but me and the cabby, who by the way, didn't know if he should stay or go. It was not at all difficult to piece together that this was their normal. Tisha and I went across the street and helped Shannette to her feet. Her lip was busted, and bleeding and her right eye was swollen shut.

Before I could think, I blurted out, *"Now how in the fuck are you going to show up on your first day Monday morning looking like this?"*

I could tell by the way she looked at me that she had completely forgotten that we were all starting at our assigned units in less than 48 hours.

There was no way that those bruises would be healed by then; if anything, she would look worse by Monday. The knock at the door didn't sound friendly at all, it sounded like it had some authority behind it.

Tisha checked the peephole and then backed up while opening the door. There were two police officers, the Hispanic female instantly went to help Nette and took pictures of her injuries. The black male officer, Sergeant Yardly, walked straight in the house towards the kitchen, like he expected Mr. Rutledge to be in there. He looked around and then said that he wanted to talk to me and to Tisha about the events leading up to the assault.

If I didn't know any better, I would swear that Sergeant Yardly had been in this house before. Although he was a seasoned officer, he seemed really familiar with Nette and her husband's shenanigans. Employed with the police department for 19 years and as the lapel on his shirt pin said, "Army Veteran", Sergeant Yardly a well -respected senior police officer had the presence of authority when he entered the room. Now the other officer, hispanic female...last name was Murillo, she was short and curvy, with jet black hair pulled pack into a ponytail. You could tell from a mile away with her no-nonsense attitude, that she didn't play.

But you could also tell that she had a soft spot for issues related to domestic violence.

She instructed the paramedics on where attention was needed on the multiple injuries, as Tisha and I were separated by Officer Yardly into different parts of the house to write our witness statements.

I wrote my statement on the dining room table and Tisha was put in a back bedroom to write hers. When we were done, Officer Yardly took the statements and looked over them. He then asked Mrs. Rutledge to write a victim's statement.

It was obvious that she was pretending to be too injured to be able to write a statement, but she promised that she would go to the police station in the morning and do it.

Without missing a beat, Officer Yardly said loud enough for everyone to hear,

"Look, if you want to keep being a fucking punching bag, don't call us out here and then not press charges. In the morning... if you're not dead... bring your ass to the station and fill out a victim statement and get an emergency protective order or don't... but we can't help you if you're gonna poke the bear and run with the stick in your hand!"

I laughed out loud out of pure shock. I did not expect that reaction at all, especially from a police officer. Officer Yardly was about 50 years old, a stocky black man with a nice build. You could tell that he worked out and took good care of himself.

You could also tell that he had been around the block a time or two with domestic violence victims and they usually don't want to write a statement. Out of fear, out of love, out of guilt, out of loyalty and sometimes out of stupidity.

"Ok, Ok, I'll do it." Shannette said, reaching for the papers to fill out.

I couldn't tell if Officer Yardly's words had gotten to her, or if she knew that her husband would be back as soon as that cop car was no longer in front of their house. Either way, It didn't take much convincing for her to figure out that a no trespass order, coupled with an emergency protection order would buy her some time to get a plan in motion and flee to safety. As the paramedics were putting away their supplies, Officer Yardly asked me to come and speak with him in the kitchen, away from everyone else.

"This one is yours, right?"

He asked, holding up my witness statement. *"Yes, Sir. Is there something wrong with it?"*

Excited he shook his head and said,

"Quite the opposite, it's a very good, detailed report, do you have formal law enforcement training?"

"Oh well, Sir, I know how to write reports, if that's what you're asking. I worked for the Department of Juvenile Justice in Queens New York for three years before moving to Texas and I'm also Army veteran, so yes, I'm very familiar with writing reports. Thanks for the compliment. Rutledge and I just graduated from the corrections academy yesterday. I rambled as I pointed to Rutledge. *We were supposed to be out celebrating when all of this happened."*

"I knew I heard a New York accent!" Officer Yardly said. Then it was like a delayed realization when he said, *"Wait, the victim is a corrections officer?"* I nodded my head up

and down as I said, "We both are, literally graduated yesterday. "I said.

He looked in her direction and shook his head in disappointment. I was correct, he was very familiar with Mr. And Mrs. Rutledge and their marital problems.

He and his partner had responded to this address plenty of times before, and Rutledge didn't fill out a victim statement any of those times before.

Officer Yardly handed me his business card as he said,

"Your report writing skills are impressive, if you ever decide on a career as a police officer, contact me. We would love to have you. Oh, and by the way, cut her ass off, she's going to get herself killed and get you caught up in her bullshit, she's a bad influence, stay away from her. I mean it!"

Officer Yardly didn't have to tell me twice. Tonight's events were crystal clear, once I understood everything. Why Shannette was unhappily married, why Mr. Rutledge didn't trust her to go out without him and why the officer yelled at her about filling out a victim's statement.

Officer Yardly and Officer Murillo left a hell of an impression on me the way that they conducted business. They were stern, but they cared and while none of us condoned the actions of Mr. Rutledge, we all agreed, that what Shannette Rutledge did tonight was not safe or wise at all.

I put the officer's business card in my purse, gave Shannette a hug and said goodbye. Tisha walked me out to my car and said that she was only in town to see her sister graduate and planned on trying to convince Nette to go back to Florida with her for her own safety. I agreed that sounded like the best option for her. I gave Tisha a hug and told her that I was glad that neither one of us had to deal with tonight's disaster alone, got in my car and slowly headed home.

That was twenty years ago, Rutledge and I never communicated again after that day. I felt bad for her, although she made a poor choice that night, she was still the victim of domestic violence at the end of the day. I heard from Tisha around the holidays, I wasn't surprised that Rutledge never relocated with her, instead she stayed with Real Ike after that incident. That level of toxicity is simply too dangerous to be around, for anybody.

Chapter 8

Magic Trick G.G.

I wasn't even on "The Row" six months when I responded to my first suicide attempt. I had only been in Texas eleven months by this point and still had my Brooklyn mentality when it came to situations or dealing with people. Offender Gilliams was a white female convict that swore she was a black woman from the hood. Her mannerisms and personal choice to avoid using proper english made you think she was from a different upbringing, but that's what prison will do to you. She would tell a new convict, upon meeting them for the first time:

"I'm Gerri, last name is Gilliams, like Williams but with a G because I'm a Gee...so call me G.G.!"

Every single time she told somebody that corny ass shit, they would laugh, raise their eyebrows and say, *"Alrighty then!!"*

She had 4 cornrows going straight back and walked the yard like a dude in an outfit that was wayyy too big.

Now, you let an Officer call her name out for a family visit and she would perform a magic trick in ten minutes flat. Gilliams would take that 2X uniform off, dig under her mattress where the stiffness of the mattress acted as an "iron", pull out that size medium, which was her actual size and take out her braids. As soon as she would apply some lipstick and eyeliner, her entire walk would go from a strut to a girly switch. The girls in the dorm would crack up and tease,

"Oh shit there go G.G. performing her magic trick, I bet her husband is here!"

Gilliams would smirk knowing she was about to enter her transformation station, as she called the handicap stall. She spent most of her days being a husband herself so watching her walk out the door with crinkly hair and a tight uniform on, if you were a new officer, you would swear she was someone else. Well today, of all days, Gilliams was in for a little rude awakening. That day seemed so ordinary, nothing crazy was going on...but as life would have it...after today, nothing would ever be ordinary ever again. Gilliams had been running so much game with multiple women in different dorms over the years. However, today, her days of playing games would come back to haunt her.

Many of the offenders on the unit were serving anywhere from 25 to life, 30–60-year sentences, some had 80-year sentences, there were quite a few that had life with parole, without parole, double life sentences and death sentences. Being honest, the ones with the death sentence were the easiest ones to work with, they pretty much knew their fate. Pretty much, they were just waiting on a dinner date with the needle. It was the 25 to life or the ones that had a chance at parole that were a real pain in the ass. Anything above 50 years was just a ball of anger walking around, waiting for a reason to explode. In theory, they didn't have a death sentence, but they knew that they were going to die in prison. I mean, shit that's 3rd grade math, 40 plus 80, meant never walking out alive again, on any calculator and in any language.

That group of offenders had nothing to lose and nothing to gain. They broke the rules, had brutal fights and did not respect authority, at all! I remember telling a convict that I was going to write her up for possession of contraband. Now being a new boot, I heard the other officers say it and saw that the threat would make them chill out. It really would depend on the situation. Well, that shit didn't work with Offender Perry, she said,

"Officer, you think I give a fuck about that write up? What are they gonna do, add another day to my 80 years?"

She laughed a laugh that reminded me of the end of Michael Jackson's Thriller. What can you say that would even matter, at that point?

A lot of the older prisoners, convicts as we called them would tell the new ones coming in,

"Whatever you do, don't shit where you sleep."

Now, I've heard the term…

"don't shit where you eat"…

but *"where you sleep"*….that was a first for me. We all know that the latter meant don't date someone in the workplace. But that prison cliché meant, if you wanna close your eyes at night without getting shanked, don't play with somebody's heart in the same dorm that you live in. Now, Gilliams knew this rule, she was on the unit a solid 12 years by the time I started working there. One of the things about an old school convict, they are just used to doing things the old school way, period. If it's new and its fancy...count them out!

Gilliams managed to have a young and cute piece of eye candy all over the unit...or as she would refer to them as her "sugar babies". She had one in damn near every dorm. A-dorm, B-dorm, a new one in C-dorm, the same dorm she's in and she even had one in G-dorm. With her job in the kitchen as a cook, she was able to move around this super maximum-security prison as if she had her own set of keys.

Gilliams was well known to all of the Officers, the rank and even the Warden. She could cook her ass off without a recipe card and if an inspection was going to happen, you made sure that Gilliams was on your roster. She was the closest thing you could get to an officer, without the uniform, the handcuffs and oh yeah, the murder conviction. When Gilliams was done with her strip search at the visitation room, she started to walk to the right when Officer Galvan told her,

"Gilliams, your visit is on the left side today".

Surprised, she sharply turned in the other direction unaware of what would be meeting her around the wall. The visitation building was set up in a way that contact visits were to the right and non-contact visits were to the left. On the right, you could hug and kiss your loved ones, your children could sit on your lap and there was no partition between you. The left side was for death row inmates mostly, but also for attorney visits and anyone not listed as a family member. When Gilliams passed the privacy wall, she could see her husband and a younger African-American man sitting to his left. His briefcase was opened and facing towards them. Gilliams smiled nervously and said,

"Hey babe!" While her eyes went back and forth from her husband of 13 years to the stranger at the table with him.

Mr. Gilliams looked away and the stranger knew that this was his cue to introduce himself.

"Mrs. Gilliams, hello, I'm Mr. Gregory Duverglass, your husband's attorney. I would shake your hand, but well you know, as he pointed to the plexiglass between them. On behalf of my client Mr. Gilliams, I am hereby notifying you that a petition for divorce will be filed with the courts Monday morning."

The air had evaporated out of Gilliams lungs, and she didn't say one word, the tears spoke for themselves. She stared at her soon-to-be ex-husband as he looked out the window and ignored her pleading eyes.

"Divorce?" was all that she could process.

THE BLACKEST BLUE

"My client has received several letters from a woman incarcerated at this facility, who in fact received... what in the eyes of the law would be considered a "love letter" from you.

This woman wrote to my client, your husband, saying that she was in love with you! This person maintains that you are taking good care of her in here and that Mr. Gilliams should stop coming up here to visit you because... well umm, when he does, you have to pretend to love him and dress like a girl."

Unable to confirm or deny such accurate and embarrassing accusations. Gilliams just began to blink rapidly, she slowly turned red and then cried silently. In other words, Ol' magic trick G.G. had performed her final act, but unfortunately no one was clapping.

"Mrs. Gilliams, is this your handwriting?"

Mr. Duverglass asked, not caring about her tears, but keeping continuing with the business as planned. When she focused her eyes, and lowered the handkerchief filled with tears, she could see the "introductory grooming letter" that she had been using over and over on so many different prisoners in the last 12 years. It literally could have been _anyone_, she thought to herself. There had to be at minimum,

40-50 duplicates of that exact same paper floating all over the prison from the nameless and forgotten about women that she thought were cute at first sight. She also considered if it was one of the few that had already gone home on parole over the last 12 years. The thought of that needle in the haystack made her anxiety flare up. For years Gilliams would fold the "introductory love letter" real small and stick it under her armpit, using deodorant as an adhesive. As she would see the "fresh meat" coming into the chow hall, they would get a peanut butter and jelly sandwich with a side of deodorant-soaked love and admiration, courtesy of Geraldine Gilliams…but the note, what prisoners would call a "kite" in their world, would always be autographed, "From your new friend G.G."

She would tell that same lie to every woman in receipt of her kite. Most of them fell for her duplicated game and just like that, she was the main attraction on the rec yard. Worked like a charm every time!

"Now before you answer that question, Mr. Duverglass continued, "I have a letter with me that YOU sent to Mr. Gilliams and the handwriting is exactly the same, I mean, I'm no forensic handwriting expert, but can you see where I'm going with this?" he said sarcastically.

Gilliams will no longer be the rooster in the hen house, there would be no more confidence in her strut on the rec yard or her cooking abilities. Gilliams was caught red handed, meek and defeated. She was also unable to think of a logical explanation in the moment.

At this point in the visit, Mr. Gilliams had basically had enough. In his mind...he accomplished what he set out to do. Which was to let her see the pain that she caused in his heart. As her husband stood up, Mr. Duverglass put the documents back in his briefcase, as if their exit was scripted.

"We're only here so that you do what's best and make things easier for Joseph."

My God, she hadn't even thought about how devastating this would be for Joseph! She looked at her husband and with everything she could muster she whispered,

"You promised!"

Mr. Gilliams closed his eyes, and G.G. watched a single tear fall down his cheek. He owed her, big time and he knew it.

She had 3 years left before she was eligible for parole and if all went well, with a letter of recommendation from the Warden and the kitchen Captain, Gilliams would try to get approved on her first shot at parole.

THE BLACKEST BLUE

Gilliams didn't walk around here being reliable and helpful to the officers for nothing. I'd never met a convict that did anything for the staff and didn't expect *something* in return. So, trust me when I tell you, if nothing else, she calculated every move she made. Chess, not checkers!

Chapter 9

Wedding Rings & Razor Blades

r. Gilliams was hurt and upset, hell…he had every right to be, but he was forgetting a promise that he made 13 years ago. Eighty-seven days before they were married, Geraldine Smith was an ER trauma nurse at Brookdale Hospital, single with no children, she was on duty one night when her team was alerted that a drunk driver hit a sedan head-on. There were three patients headed their way in ambulances with lights and sirens blaring. As things were explained to them, the drunk driver was in serious condition, but the elderly couple was in grave condition. She saw a man running in the ER doors within minutes and frantically inquiring about his parents.

She made contact with Leo Gilliams, the son of the elderly couple and it was evident that he was devastated by the news of his parents' condition. Within hours of their arrival, Leo's dad passed away and Nurse Smith was on duty when he needed someone to comfort him. Being the prominent businessman that he was, Leo had his staff hold all calls and allow him to grieve. For the next four days he visited with his mom, and he would ask for Nurse Smith if he didn't see her. When she went home, they would talk for hours. Soon, they were on a first name basis, and she would be crossing professional and ethical lines. The following week, on her day off, Gerri got a call from one of her colleagues... Mrs. Gilliams had also passed away. She rushed to the hospital to be with him for comfort. Seeing Leo overwhelmed with grief, Gerri was noticeably heartbroken.

Wishing she could do something to ease his sorrow, Gerri started to become extremely attached to the grieving son and more detached from her co-workers. It had been speculated that someone mysteriously mixed up the medication for the IV that would be injected into the arm of the drunk driver.

THE BLACKEST BLUE

Although they would never admit to it, it was rumored that she killed the drunk driver to ease the pain of the man she was falling in love with. She was convicted of murder, by way of circumstantial evidence. That day, that the drunk driver mysteriously coded, Nurse Smith was seen on the 4th floor, by a cleaning lady, minutes before the "Code Blue" was called. Feeling indebted to her, after burying both of his parents. Mr. Gilliams proposed to Nurse Smith, which surprised everyone.

Unfortunately, that proposal drew the attention of the authorities and Gerri became their prime suspect. Before the trial date was set, they were married and she would give birth to a baby boy, named Joseph.

He was a newborn when she was convicted and in all of these years, they have managed to hold on to hope and make things work. Well, that was until she forgot her role as a wife and lost sight of who and what was more important, her image to be known around the unit as a man or to get her shit together and become a productive member of society? When Gilliams went back to her dorm, the feeling of betrayal was an understatement. She didn't want to show her hand and let it be known that her visit went horribly wrong. She didn't even bother to ask the attorney to confirm the identity of the sender. By process of elimination, she pretty much knew who sent the letters to her husband. It had to be the chick in her same dorm, but she also knew that a confrontation would only end badly for her chances with parole. The crazy thing is that there were no signs that it was the girl in her dorm...like zero.

Fifteen minutes after she returned from her visit, an emergency response team was called to C-dorm, the same dorm that Gilliams was assigned to. All of the offenders were evacuated and on the prison response team was Captain Gaines, Sergeant Vaughn, three officers, me and the medical staff. When we entered the bathroom to help Offender Gilliams, she looked like someone had thrown her against a red wall that was freshly painted. There was blood everywhere and she kept clearing her throat but wouldn't talk. Another offender had already wrapped pieces of cloth and paper towel around her wrists and applied pressure until we got there.

Running with Gilliams in a wheelchair, we passed the Multi-Purpose Facility and into the doors of the infirmary. Mr. Fleming, the head of the medical department was waiting with Lieutenant Hampton for us to arrive and instantly he said,

"Ok, roll the camera for my briefing."

THE BLACKEST BLUE

Now remember, I haven't even been on the unit a full year yet and I still have that raw Brooklyn mentality. Mr. Fleming points to the officer holding the handheld camera to signal that he was ready to go live,

" And Go!" Officer Wilson said.

"This is Medical Supervisor Fleming, the date is...January 2nd, the time now is 2:13pm, I am in the Infirmary with Offender Geraldine Gilliams, ID number 96A0582, Offender Gilliams has made a suicide attempt in which it appears that she made some cuts across both wrists with a sharp object, corrections staff has conducted a full search of Offender Gilliams' person, the bathroom stall and her personal property.

At this time, I am going to remove the bandages and access for the need of stitches or if we need a transport team to the local hospital. Officers have been unsuccessful in finding the razor blade and Offender Gilliams will not communicate with us."

Just as he said that Offender Gilliams cleared her throat and in a low raspy tone, she said,

"I swallowed it."

Not one person panicked or even found this alarming, they were so used to this behavior that she might as well had said, *"Nice day today."* Mr. Fleming, with his professional bedside manner, never missed a beat, he ordered one of the medical staff to get some bread from the refrigerator and he told Officer Wilson to keep the camera rolling.

As he handed her the bread to push the razor down that was stuck in her throat, he began to carefully remove the cloth wrapped around her wrists. Mr. Fleming poured saline solution on her wrists, and once we all had a clear view, you could see about 10 superficial papercuts going across her wrist like a bunch of gold bracelets.

And that was the moment, right there when I said some dumb rookie shit.

"Pwahhahaa, girl you wasn't tryna kill yourself with them lil slices, if you really wanted to kill yourself you would have cut deep and long like this, not across."

As I demonstrated a vertical cutting motion from my wrist and up to my forearm. I swear the room stopped and everyone in the room stopped breathing and blinking. You could hear a mouse peeing on a cotton ball, I swear! Mr. Fleming looked dead at me and said,

"You! In my office. Now!!"

THE BLACKEST BLUE

Camera still rolling, he excused himself and quickly walked into his office, and I followed with my dumb rookie ass. In low tones through gritted teeth he said,

"What the hell was that!!?? Don't you EVER, advise an inmate on how to commit suicide and you damn sure don't do it with the camera rolling!!

As he smacks his own forehead in disbelief.

My eyes were buck like a rockstar on cocaine...while I was being scolded.

"Everybody out there is white", he continued, *"You and I are the only black ones in the room and you gonna say that!!!??? Don't let that happen again!" I'll deal with them; you just keep your mouth shut!"*

"Yes, Sir"

Was all I could say, with my stupid ass.

I was so embarrassed, but grateful, because Mr. Fleming handled me professionally and schooled me at the same time.

As if it was planned, the minute we re-entered the room, Gilliams coughed up the razor, which distracted everyone from my unprofessional debut. When an offender is suicidal, immediately, they are placed in a room that has freezing temperatures for 72 hours, naked. The theory is, if you want

89

to hurt yourself, that's all you'll think about. But, if you're freezing cold, the only thing you will think about is how to stay warm. Not about suicide.

As simple as it seems, it worked every time. After 24 hours of compliance, you can earn a suicide smock. It's a weighted vest styled dress with 3 large Velcro strips across the back. It goes on the offender just like a hospital gown, backwards. Each time that they need to use the restroom, you can open the food chute and count off 10 squares of toilet tissue for them to use. Never would you ever give a suicidal person the entire roll of tissue. Believe it or not, the creativity to use whatever items necessary to commit suicide is alarming.

By the 48th hour of good behavior in the ice box, you are now given a suicide blanket, made of the same rip-proof material as the smock. Both are the ugliest color of booger green known to man and never to be confused as a fashion statement. Hideous to say the least. But effective.

Chapter 10

30 Years to Death

he entire time they're in the single cell set-up, Officers conduct a 15-minute observation and account for signs of life. Gilliams spent her 72 hours in the butt naked think box and returned to her dorm after being cleared by medical. For security reasons, her property was packed up and stored in the Lieutenant's office. In 12 years, no one had ever seen Gilliams behave that way, many others have attempted, some were successful, but she was the talk of the unit for about a week. As the months went on, the seasons changed and more offenders came in, but rarely did any leave.

THE BLACKEST BLUE

I was assigned to A-dorm when I was approached by a black offender in her late 50's to early 60's. She had two black and white composition notebooks in her hand as she approached my desk.

"Well Officer, do you have any entries for my books?"

She asked. It wasn't that I didn't know what she meant, she had been walking around with those books for six months, filling the pages in with advice from every aspect of life. I said,

"Let me see what you have so far."

As I read though the entries, I had to catch my own facial expressions because what seemed to be funny, and shocking at first became more realistic, depressing and sadder. Offender Jackson had been in prison for over 30 years, flat, day for day since 1975. She was about to be released in a few weeks, and she was overjoyed at her second chance at life. In those two books were things for her to experience, movies to watch, places to go and foods to try.

Hundreds upon thousands of the things we take for granted, were things that she had missed out on ...for over thirty years!! As I looked at the different handwritten entries, I blurted out

"You didn't see Star Wars!!?"

"Ghostbusters!!??"

"You missed the entire VHS era!!??

"You never used spray deodorant!!??

"Wait! You never used a microwave before??"

She just smiled, shook her head and softly said,

"No, Ma'am, been here since 1975, I missed out on quite a bit."

The gravity of that statement was uncomfortable, I couldn't tell if it was because she was in the car and never actually entered the bank when it was robbed or because 1975 was the year I was born. But either way, this was deep. I added 2 entries and wished her well. I wrote:

"Go to New York City!"

"Eat Pizza when you get to Brooklyn."

Life on Death Row... has got to be the most profound oxymoron known to man, but it's a real thing. When an offender is given their date, the news travels like a feather in a tornado. It was Franny Newt who was up next to be executed by the State of Texas. The Warden allowed her to pick the officers she wanted on her death watch.

What that would mean for the selected officers, is that they would position themselves outside of her cell for their entire 8-hour shift. The only items allowed down the wing of "The Row" directly in front of her cell would be an old school elementary chair with the attached desk, a pen and a logbook, their lunch and something to drink. As she moved around conducting daily activities, our job was to annotate what she was doing...precisely.

Logbook entry- 3:11pm Offender Newt is eating a snack.

Logbook entry- 3:13pm Offender Newt is brushing her teeth.

Logbook entry- 3:17pm Offender Newt is washing her face.

Logbook entry- 3:23pm Offender Newt is sitting on her bunk, listening to music on her radio.

Literally everything, including any trips to the shower or the toilet. Selected meant you were respected and well-liked by the offenders on "The Row". In other words, nobody wants a fucking bitch sitting outside of their cell right before they're scheduled to die by lethal injection, period!

The theory was that a person would become more suicidal in the two weeks prior their execution date than they had been throughout the long wait to get an execution date. It's been said, their logic is, instead of letting the state "take them out", they would rather take themselves out. So, to avoid a situation from happening, there is 24 hour, up close and personal monitoring, completed in 8-hour shifts by 3 officers a day, for 2 weeks before the execution date.

Nine officers were selected by Offender Newt personally for death watch duty, and then 2 separate officers were selected to accompany her on the ride in the van to the Polunsky Unit in Huntsville, Texas. Now the officers are not permitted to actually watch the execution, but they take the ride, drop her off, turn around and come back. That's where the shit really goes down, the gurney, the priest, the last meal, the needle...the end.

Franny Newt sat at the edge of her bunk as I secured the leg irons around her ankles. She let out a sigh as she slowly stood up. While I secured the belly chain and handcuffs, she continued to stare down at her feet. It was evident why she hated the mandatory policy on being handcuffed and shackled when taking a shower... behind a closed door... in a secured building... surrounded by layers and layers of barbed wire...with officers in towers holding rifles and shotguns...in a super maximum-security prison, from inside of the shower where could she logically run to? That just made absolutely no sense to anyone. There were 8 women on death row in 2005, and it had been well over 10 years since the last woman was executed. Somber was the forecast and gloomy was the prediction for the next few days to come.

Chapter 11

The Row

Most of the women were nice, although at one moment in their lives, they did some crazy shit. Some stories had even the news, they had a community within a community, but just like any nice neighborhood, there was always one rotten apple to spoil the bunch. Words like, pest, annoying, pain in the ass, wicked witch, and Jesus Christ would she just go the fuck to sleep...came to my mind often when I thought of the state's tenant in cell #4.

Melinda McCarty was the broken light bulb at the end of a graffiti filled urine-soaked tunnel. Being nice took too much effort and for her it was so much easier to ruin your day if the opportunity presented itself. If she was awake, the opportunity always presented itself.

She would do dumb shit like, count the grains of rice on her tray every day and write the date and the total number next to it, just to fuck with the kitchen Captain about fairness and consistency.

Offender McCarty would grieve the color of the wind, the sound of the rain and any day of the week that ended in "y". Whatever you do, please don't talk too loud at the officer's station. For sure she was like a tape recorder with Energizer batteries. This bitch just kept on going and going!

"Officer, I want a grievance", was literally on constant repeat. Words like please and thank you, escaped her vocabulary daily and literally took too much energy to use. I wouldn't attribute her rudeness to her upbringing, if I had to sum it up, I would say she was mean for sport. Whenever McCarty had a visit from her son, he was always pleasant, the perfect gentleman, and nothing like his mother. At least there was some hope for her bloodline.

Everyone in a 400-mile radius was aware that in 2 days, Franny Newt was going to take the ride down to Huntsville. For days it had been eerily quiet on "The Row".

With all of her prison jewelry on, I escort Franny Newt out of her cell. I have my left hand cupped to the back of Offender Newt's right arm just in case she trips in those shackles around her ankles. As we passed by McCarty cell, morbidly obese, and mad at the world, she's standing at the door, holding onto the bars with the pure look of evil on her face as a moisturizer. I couldn't believe my ears as McCarty sinister voice pierced our eardrums as we walked by.

"Hey Newt, tick tock, tick tock, Ahahhahhaha!"

"Knock it off McCarty*!!"* I ordered.

Brianna Goldberg one of the women on Death Row, mostly known for her brains and her beauty, yelled from her cell on the other side of The Row, "Shut your fucking hole, Bitch!!"

But it was too late, the damage had already been done. Franny Newt held her focus and never looked bothered, but I knew that stung like an Ali punch. Especially coming from another black woman facing the same fate, it was just all kinds of fucked up. But to be honest, every black officer was embarrassed by McCarty's behavior. Everything was about race with her, even with black officers. If you didn't give her what she wanted, it was because she was black, even if the officer was black too. Now make that shit make sense.

She would put on an academy award performance for white officers and that shit used to make my skin crawl. Mid-day and evening visits were a normal thing for offenders on death row, never in the morning like the others. Newt was able to shake off that jab and get ready for one of her last visits before the big day. Once the visit was over, I asked Offender Newt about the slim, dark and handsome man that was waving goodbye, blowing kisses and crying.

"Oh, Nate, awww, he's been my boyfriend for the last 6 years now. He's gotten me through this horrible time. I swear he came out of nowhere. He started off as my pen pal and then started sending pictures. Didn't hurt that he was cute too." She giggled.

We had gotten so used to the routine of things, Offender Newt had managed to undress, squat and cough, show me the backs of her feet, lift her breasts and continue talking, all while smiling at the thought of finding love again.

"He knew about my case and didn't judge me, he even asked me to marry him 2 years ago, but I said no...I just didn't see no point in it, whether we loved each other or not."

Nathaniel Blackmon was a decent looking man. A widower for the last ten years, he had lost his wife in a car accident, she was drunk behind the wheel and hit a tree, Newt explained. His family understood that he was probably lonely and could see why he didn't pass judgement on anyone, to include Franny Newt. He thought that making Franny his wife would make her heart come alive again, but after being found guilty of executing her infant children and her husband for insurance money, Franny Newt was barely alive since she was sentenced to death by lethal injection, back in 1989.

"Take care of my girl".

Nate said as his eyes locked with mine. I nodded, as if I had any say over her upcoming execution. We both knew I didn't. I handed him back his driver's license and buzzed the door to the exit. *"Take care of yourself Mr. Blackmon"*, was the only thing that came to my head, because *"have a nice day"* just wasn't going to work for this situation.

Walking out of the door that day, he knew what that meant. He knew that he would never see her or talk to her again. He made the trip every single week for the last six years to be where his heart called him to be.

A few hours a week out of his life was a small sacrifice, he reasoned with himself. He wasn't completely sold on her guilt or innocence, but the State of Texas had spoken.

One day, before a log entry of a two-hour nap, Franny Newt handed me a stack of documents through her food chute. It was literally the thickness of The Yellow Pages phone book.

THE BLACKEST BLUE

Her instructions were," *I'm about to lay down for a while, I'm sure when I wake up, you'll have questions after reading this.* "

The top page read "This page intentionally left blank", when I flipped it back, the next page read,

"All rise! The Honorable Judge presiding. "

I looked at her and said, *"Holy shit".* I pointed and asked, *"Is this from your trial? "* Franny Newt nodded and laid down for her afternoon nap.

It was the transcripts from her 1988 jury trial. I read everything, made notes, cross referenced the opening statements with the closing remarks and even read the verdict. When Newt woke up from her nap, the documents were in the original position that she gave them to me in, stacked, in numerical page order. I pretended as if I had never seen those documents before in my life. I didn't ask any questions, and she didn't ask me if I had any questions. She also, pretended as if she had never handed those documents to me. We both went on as if that moment never happened. I had no questions, I understood what I read.

Before Nate could finish the pan of meatloaf that he made for this week's meal prep, the love he had known over the last few years, would have a sheet over her head and a tag on

her toe. As predicted, the clouds lingered for the ladies on The Row, long after the burial. They were all keeping busy, staying to themselves and finding books to read. Even cell #4 was quiet, which was unusual, even for her. I bet that as much as she wanted to be childish and say something sinister. She surrendered to the respected sorrow dancing in the air. She didn't ask for any grievances or argue with any officers. For once, she behaved like everyone else, an adult. I swear this will sound crazy, but it was nice to see that she could act civilized, even temporarily. It finally sunk into them. Although most of the women had arrived there after Franny Newt, this was the first time that they lost a link in their chain, in a little over a decade. Of course, the victims are thought of, the families of the victims are prayed for, even the soul on the gurney is sometimes forgiven. People often forget about the families affected by their loved one's actions, what about their pain? When the Warden over executions asked her for her last statement, she declined to say a word...to me ...that spoke volumes. She didn't want her last breath to be a lie. So, she said nothing. But everybody knows what goes through the minds of the women on death row, immediately after an execution. before they get in their steel bunk at night and as soon as they wake up each morning, day in and day out. They all wonder...
"Who's next?"

Chapter 12

Officer Needs Assistance

Word around the unit was that Officer Scott was resigning, unlike everyone else that leaves or gets fired during a scandal, her husband was taking a job in Germany as a contractor, and she would be leaving soon to travel abroad with him. We threw her a quick-going-away party and wished her the best. Jokingly, I asked the kitchen captain if I could have Scott's job once she's gone. Captain Hamlin said,

"Yeah, but not for first shift, if you come, you'll have to go to second shift".

Wait, what?? Was he serious?? Ten-hour shifts, four days a week, rotating days off. You mean I wouldn't have to be on a schedule where it's six days on shift and three days off duty.

Breaking up fights, walking in on all kinds of sex acts, coughing every time someone was getting pepper sprayed, dealing with arguments over stupid shit like a teaspoon of coffee that's missing, stolen potato chips and watching them run con games from the time their eyes open??Hell yeah! Sign me up and do it yesterday! I learned fast in my new assignment that the same con games in the dorms were the same con games in the kitchen, they just used sugar, cheese, seasoning, meat and each other to be successful. I was on my third year on "The Row" when I made the change to go in the kitchen, if for nothing else, I did it for the hours. Working 10am-6pm was nice, I could go back to sleep after dropping my daughter off to school and my son was with the sitter. Ms. Alice was great to the kids and would work around our schedule at a moment's notice.

Offender Gilliams was still in the kitchen, making magic happen in those pots. If she remembered my rookie comment from that day, she never made it known. Two things happened that day, I never made a dumb ass comment like that again, and Gilliams never wore another size 2X uniform again.

Now like I said, the con games continued, it was three officers assigned to first shift and three officers assigned to second shift. We roamed around the kitchen like ships in the night, rarely did we stand in the same location unless all of the offenders were eating in the dining area. We wanted to avoid losing our supply of hot commodities…so to keep an eye on 16 opportunists, my co-workers, Ms. King, Ms. Washington and I had to divide and conquer.

Gilliams would stand behind the serving line and watch everything coming and going. Gilliams was a completely different person after that razor blade incident. She had gone cold turkey on playing husband on the rec yard and over time, Mr. Gilliams was convinced that she had walked away from playing with heads and hearts, to include his own. He would still occasionally receive mail from someone on the unit, threatening to take back the best thing that ever happened to her.

Slowly and methodically, Gilliams tried everything she could to figure out who had betrayed her trust. Another love connection on the unit would answer the question that had gone unanswered long enough. One night, about a year after Mr. Gilliams threatened to file for a divorce, the ugly and embarrassing truth seeped out… hot and steamy, like a tea kettle. I was on night shift temporarily and all we heard was,

"Hey!! Can y'all hear me?"

"This officer needs assistance!"

Was the shaky voice over the radio. The hairs on the back of our necks stood up because we immediately knew that an inmate got their hands on an officer's radio! When you hear someone say, "and then the calvary came", this must have been the incident they were talking about. I think officers abandoned their duty posts to get to the mystery location. At 2am it was easy to hear the screams by the window coming from G-dorm. Lieutenant Hampton used her master key and let a mob of officers inside to find Officer Willis on the floor, laying in her own blood. Officer Tracie Willis had been on the unit for 7 years. A strawberry blonde officer with blue eyes and a warm smile. She would be considered petite for a woman in her late 30's/early 40's. Officer Willis was badly beaten and cut in her face with a razor.

THE BLACKEST BLUE

G-dorm housed general population offenders, half of the dorm worked in the sewing shop, creating oven mitts and chef hats with matching aprons. While the other half worked as beauticians, boot blacks, and cleaning trustees. If you were going to get complacent, this would be the dorm you would do it in. Not that you should *ever* get complacent, but this is the most harmless group of murderers, if that was ever a thing. There were 48 offenders accounted for when the emergency headcount was conducted.

Aside from the one that got up to use the bathroom and found Officer Willis, everyone else was dead asleep and had missed the horror show. It was literally a "Whodunnit?" The Warden, The Assistant Warden, The Major, The Captains and anybody who was anybody was on the scene to get to the bottom of this mess.

"Well, somebody knows something, and until somebody says something, there will be no movement in or out of G-dorm!"

That was the order from the Warden and there was nothing to negotiate. Every single one was taken to an interview area, inspected thoroughly from head to toe, strip searched and required to give a written statement. And still...nothing.

THE BLACKEST BLUE

The only person that wrote more than *"I was sleep and I didn't hear or see anything, the end"* was the one that found her.

They say never judge a book by its cover, well, I'm judging this book because there is no way that this old lady could have caused this kind of damage. She just wasn't physically capable. The kitchen was informed that they would have to adjust and instead of receiving 48 offenders from G-dorm in a cafeteria styled setting. They would need 96 johnny sacks made on the fly. The Warden was not playing! They will get cabin fever and turn on each other before she would compromise this investigation. Officer Willis was in stable condition at the local hospital, and she too said that she had no idea what happened. Her story was almost believable, except for the strands of black hair caught in her wristwatch collected as evidence.

The doctor asked that she be allowed to rest and respectfully his request was granted, but she was hiding something and as soon as those baby blue eyes opened the next morning, she had a lot of explaining to do.

THE BLACKEST BLUE

"Call in the dogs!" Warden Chasen demanded in a firm voice. The offenders had to stand near their bunk as the bloodhound sniffed the watch, then trotted and sniffed around the officer's station.

When he was done, he trotted and sniffed around the 1st toilet stall, closest to the wall and as he made his way around all of the bunks, Buddy the Bloodhound plopped down in front of Offender Lee and looked up at his handler for his treat.

"Cuff her!" Warden Chasen demanded.

Lee was escorted out of G-dorm, holding her head down as if she didn't expect to get caught. By now she knew that the truth would have to come out, she had no choice. Offender Mia Lee had a lengthy prison sentence, 60 years, for stabbing an old lady with a fork at her father's restaurant. Her anger was animalistic and yet to be managed. She's been here 10 years already, so by now, what would make her so angry??

"I'll only talk to the Warden and Lieutenant Hampton, the rest of y'all, I don't fool with, so take it or leave it!".

Lee barked as if she was in control, and everyone knew that if they wanted to hear her story, she was in control, whether they liked it or not! It was not an option how this interview was going to go, as much as the rank wanted to throw their weight around. Warden Chasen simply wasn't having it. She

THE BLACKEST BLUE

wanted to get down to the bottom of what happened, and before the Director of Prisons would reprimand her for not having things under control, she didn't have time to entertain protocol, hurt feelings or policy, point blank. Offender Lee would only talk to two people...two were way better than none.

111

Chapter 13

Solved Mysteries

"Alright, I'll tell you, everything...ok?" Lee bargained, but first let me say to both of y'all, I'm sorry and embarrassed for how I conducted myself."

Warden Chasen motioned for Lieutenant Hampton to press the red button on the video recorder. She then said,

"Ok, we're ready Lee, go ahead, tell us what happened."

They were never prepared to hear a story like this, but Lee told it ...full of emotion.

"Ma'am, I have been on this unit 10 years, you know I don't give y'all no trouble. About a year ago, I won't lie, I started

flirting with Officer Willis. I knew she wasn't no rookie, and she wouldn't write me up, not for flirting.

Shit I was thinking, I got 50 left on a 60, why not, all she could say to me is "no". But Ma'am, she didn't say no. She was acting like we really go together, like she was my wife or something, as soon as I asked her to be my girl, she was with it...right on the spot. She was bringing me food from outside and mailing letters to me and everything. I lost count on how many times we kissed or had sex when everybody went to sleep. She was falling in love hard, a little too hard for me, so after a while, I won't lie, I wanted to cut her off. She was too clingy. I don't know how, but she was getting assigned to this dorm every day, like for real, she would even come in on her days off and still get assigned in my dorm. I even tried to get written up so I could get moved and the officers just kept giving me warnings. It was crazy because it was like I could pinpoint it, around the time when she started acting funny, but I just didn't understand why.

She used to "fake search" my property box before, but all of a sudden, she was doing a shake down on my bunk every single day, even when I knew my number didn't come up for a random search. I kept telling my cellies, and all they could say was,

THE BLACKEST BLUE

*"You took a shit where you eat and you sleep, deal with it!"
but Ma'am... Tracie ...I mean, Officer Willis was overdoing
it and that shit was embarrassing for real!*

*All I know is around the summer, something in her snapped.
She went from being in love and all nice to completely evil
towards me, for nothing, I didn't do shit to her. We stopped
fooling around and everything. Like something was wrong,
she started acting crazy. Well today they did mail call before
she came in and I got a letter...nothing different from the
many letters I get from her. I was like "Here we go with the
bullshit" I was expecting another one of her bipolar letters
but this time when I opened it, it wasn't addressed to me, it
was addressed to a Mr. Gilliams! Here, look at it."*

*As Mia Lee leaned forward in her handcuffs, Warden
Chasen could see a letter in her uniform pocket with some
blood on it. Just like the offender said, written from Tracie
Willis' home address, in her handwriting, Warden Chasen's
eyes slid across the words rapidly. Masking her disbelief,
she had never expected this mess and drama to come from
one of her own!*

*"Ma'am, she was saying all kinds of shit in that letter. Lee
continued, she was threatening him about causing her to lose
G.G., but that didn't make sense. Tracie..umm, I mean
Officer Willis said that G.G. was "the love of her life". But*

THE BLACKEST BLUE

I was confused as hell because G.G. never messed with officers like that, never, in all the years I've known her! Ma'am, this idiot...your officer... put the wrong letter in my envelope! She probably sent the letter she meant to send to me to him! All this time G.G. been on the unit thinking one of us betrayed her and it was Officer Willis this whole fucking time!"

She banged her fist on the desk with each word. Rage in her eyes as the anger continued to build.

"I just snapped! I'm not sure what she told y'all, but she knew it was me that assaulted her! I confronted her with the letter when everyone was racked up in their bunks. She tried to play dumb, and when that didn't work...she insulted my intelligence with the craziest shit ever! She had the nerve to say that me and G.G. swapped letters! Can you believe that shit!? We argued about it. She was crying and asking me to lower my voice. The thing that got me was she kept saying she didn't send that letter to me. Just lying and I'm standing there with the evidence in my motherfucking hand! The envelope was addressed to me, but the letter inside was addressed to MISTER GILLIAMS...and no matter how she tried to make it work in her favor by saying we switched letters...neither one of us are Mister Gilliams! I was so mad at the hell she was putting me through with the bunk

searches every single day, doing weird shit to stress me out and then to read that she was destroying G.G.'s family too, man, that girl tried to kill herself behind this mess! I was just sick of her shit Ma'am.

This is stuff I expect from these convicts, for real, not no damn officer! Mia Lee, gave the tears in her eyes permission to fall as she said, "Warden, I got 50 years left on my sentence and I just said, "Fuck it!"

"So, yeah, I wrapped my fists up with an old raggedy shirt so there would be no marks on my hands, and I beat her ass good when she was over there at her desk falling asleep.

I won't lie, I was quiet. I had time to take the bloody wraps from my hands, flush everything down the toilet and wash up in the sink. Your officers didn't mess up trying to find me, I fell asleep for real because, I beat her ass right after headcount and y'all didn't wake us up until almost 3 hours later."

Two flies and a guitar could have fit in Lieutenant Hampton's mouth …because her mouth… was wide open!

Warden Chasen just blinked and held a straight face, but I'm sure she wanted to do more than just sit there like a statue. Maybe she was just in shock too.

If I had to guess, she had a feeling that was somewhere between anger and embarrassment.

Offender Lee sat back in the chair and exhaled like she had just smoked a Newport cigarette. Exhausted from her own story, Lee knew that she would be in trouble, she knew that any romantic involvement with an officer would end in her transfer to another facility. The next morning when Officer Willis opened her eyes, she was handcuffed to the hospital bed and read her Miranda rights.

Offenders: 1   Officers: 0

We were looking really bad on the news and even worse in the newspapers. Willis had managed to wreak havoc on that unit, out of pure boredom. Just doing shit for sport, the consequences didn't even matter to her.

Officer Willis had never been romantically involved with Gilliams, let alone in love with her. She was never the recipient of the duplicated love letters floating around the unit. But one summer, as fate would have it, searching Lee's cell for the umpteenth time, she stumbled upon those meaningless lines written 11 years ago to Mia Lee because she was fresh meat in the chow line.

Long before Officer Willis ever worked there. Lee and Gilliams had a little thing going on. They went back and forth, meeting in the rec yard and passing kites for a few months. Not long after that, G.G. was on to her next victim. If Lee did anything wrong...it was three things:

~She got into a romantic relationship with an officer.

~She assaulted an officer... and

~11 years ago, she kept a kite that she should have thrown away.

There was that feather in the tornado again. By the time the news got to G.G., she handled it like a soldier. Mainly because Warden Chasen and Lieutenant Hampton knew that professionally it would be best to sit her down and tell her all of the details as they knew them. This would stop a falsehood on the gossip train from entering her station. She was awakened in the early morning hours to be taken to the Warden's office. Stuff like this is usually a death notice and G.G. was on pins and needles wondering what kind of bad news was headed her way. Never in a million years would she have guessed that the mystery that bothered her soul daily would finally surface to the top and make more sense than all of the other scenarios she had imagined. The fact that her con games had come back full circle to bite her in the ass was the complete opposite of what she thought.

For the first time in a long time, she did more listening than she did talking. She honestly felt relief that this would be over soon, especially after the warden asked G.G. to call her husband. The Warden herself explained the entire situation from start to finish, she didn't add anything or forget to explain anything in full detail. She also sent her sincere apologies for the actions of the former officer. In the event a lawsuit would be looming in the midst, Warden Chasen wanted to protect TDCJ as best as she could from that liability. Within a week, the feather was swirling and twisting in a different direction and G.G. stayed focused on trying to make parole.

I walked over to the ODR, which stood for, Officers Dining Room and checked on Offender McClennan, who was in her zone. Aside from the planned meals listed throughout the month on the calendar, McClellan was what you would consider a short order cook. At the request of any officer on their break, she would whip up a cheeseburger with all of the fixings, a hot dog, fries or even a fresh grilled cheese sandwich. She never made the tea sweet enough for me, but 1 more yellow packet of sweetener always did the trick. She had the job in the ODR for a solid 4 years and was good at what she did. McClellan was in her late 40's...I would give her 48 but not a day older than that. I didn't know much about her, but her personality fit the job. She must have either worked as a waitress or in retail because she really went above and beyond with customer service.

Thanksgiving was coming and there was a shift in the energy on the unit. I remember 3 years ago when I first started, I would hear that Thanksgiving and Christmas were hard to work, not because we would rather be home without own families, but because the suicide attempts and the amount of depression would be at an all-time high. I beg to differ, in my logical opinion, not everyone celebrates Christmas, some for religious reasons and some don't because they don't have good childhood memories of the holiday. Foster care or homelessness made December 25th come and go without toys or Santa in some families. Thanksgiving and New Years was the same way, some loved it and to some, it was just another day like Valentine's Day and Labor Day. I will work any of those holidays...but I will never, ever work Mother's Day! That day...is the worst day to work, because EVERYBODY misses their mom! Well, except for the ones that killed theirs...but let's stay on track.

Chapter 14

Convictions and Consequences

*M*en, women, juveniles, murderers, rapists, drug dealers, bank robbers, child abductors…everyone. They cry from sunrise to sunset, whether their mom is alive or deceased. The men cry or sleep all day because they either miss their mom, their grandmother or their wife. The women cry because they either miss their mom, grandmother, Godmother, favorite aunt, sister or they are a mom themselves and miss their children. But wait a damn minute!

THE BLACKEST BLUE

You are not ready for the arguments between the offender in bunk 12 that love and miss her children...as she wakes up next to the offender in bunk 13 that killed her children.... lord have mercy, it's ugly. As soon as it starts getting close to Mother's Day, all you hear is,

"Bitch, I better not see one motherfucking tear fall out your eyes on Sunday Bitch because I miss mine and you killed yours Bitch!

Non-stop bickering, arguing and lots of fights. The stress level is on a million around Mother's Day, and truth be told, these same people didn't give two shits about Father's Day.

Every year, the same drill. I take off every year on Mother's Day...that first year working with Juveniles was not cool and the tears got worse in every facility after...the build up to that day you can keep it. I learned the hard way about that day.

I get to work thinking today would be like any other day when Captain Hamlin said,

"They're short staffed on the unit today, I need one of y'all to work on the unit as a rover."

Rover responsibilities keep you outside monitoring movement on the unit, pat searches and strip searches are done by the Rover when the level 4 and 5 offenders go to the chow hall. They also escort to and from the library where college classes are held. These women with long sentences are getting associate degrees, learning skilled trades like braille so that they can create books for the blind. Yep, they are bettering themselves with the hopes to walk out of this condemned place one day and slide back into society as if they never left.

Lieutenant Hampton radioed me to come to her office. When I got there, she handed me two red mesh bags that's normally used for commissary and asked me to go the Chapel. I was to inform offender Jones, the Chaplain's assistant, that she was getting transferred to another unit, I was to give her the red bags and escort her everywhere until she was completely packed. I thought I would tell her, and she would go pack her property and that would be it. But of course, that's not how it went, and at this point I am convinced that I'm a shit magnet.

Jenny Jones became unglued, right there in the Chapel. Crying and hyperventilating. She kept whispering the same thing under her breath, over and over.

"I'll have to start all over, no one is going to accept me, they'll bring up my case and I'll have to go through this all over again!"

She wasn't talking directly to me; she was just talking out loud and panicking. The one thing that is a gift and a curse when working at the prison, is that you have no clue what their crimes are.

There's no computer at the desk to research their names or look up their cases, no Google, no Snapped episodes...this was during AOL dial-up. The only thing we had at work was a roster on a clipboard and a logbook. You could literally be in the same room as 48 women charged with murder and not even know it. You literally couldn't tell the difference between the ones that are guilty by association or the ones that are actually doing the time for the crime that they committed themselves. I asked a veteran who worked there for over 15 years, Sergeant Tuggle was assigned to night shift and every so often she would do overtime on day shift.

I knew it would be safe to ask her, she was cool with officers and didn't play with the inmates at all.

"What is Jenny Jones convicted of, I told her she was going to another unit and she damn near had a stroke?"

As she gave me a side eye she asked, "You don't know what she did! How long have you been working here?"

"4 years" I answered proudly like it was an accomplishment.

She said *"Shit, you're still new! You might not be ready yet "new boot" but let me school you right quick. If ever, the conversation comes up and an offender feel comfortable enough to tell you what they did...DO NOT make a comment, look shocked or act like you just heard some crazy shit. If you can do that, then you MIGHT be ready! They'll eventually tell you, you just have to figure out how to get them to talk, trust me, once you get them talking, they will tell you every detail, almost like they couldn't wait to get it off their chest or something."*

"Got it, thanks!" I said...all excited like I had some new instructions or something.

That night I went home and searched for the name Jenny Jones on my desktop computer ... why in the hell did I do that? Jones was a pediatric nurse, charged with killing over 65 babies in 3 different hospital nurseries that she worked in. The sickening part was that she was only a nurse for one year! I'm glad that I found the information while I was at home because I practiced my poker face when I pressed the enter button....and I failed miserably.

My mouth flew open, and I said "Oh my God" out loud. As soon as that slipped out, I thought of Sergeant Tuggle's instructions.

I began researching some of the names that I remembered and by the time I finished looking up all the women on The Row, I had perfected my poker face.

I remembered one woman that was on death row, offender Darlene Rogers. She showed me her transcript from trial on one of my days sitting on death watch for Franny Newt. Out of all of the women there, she was the only one that I honestly believed was not guilty of what she was convicted of. I saw photos of her injuries that were not admissible into evidence during her trial, and I was not convinced that she killed all 3 of her little girls. Somebody did it, but it wasn't her, not with that gash across her throat, and the places where she had big black and blue marks…you literally can't do that to yourself. Somebody killed her babies and tried to kill her too. But it wasn't her!

You learn really fast that you can't have an opinion on their crimes as an officer, biggest conflict of interest known to man because the ones that are guilty as fuck like Belinda McCarty will look you dead in your face and cry as she tells you a bold face lie.

When I returned to work, Gilliams pulled me to the side and said,

"Did that baby killer nurse really get sent to another unit?"

I said sharply, *"Why are you asking me?"*

"It's all over the unit that you had her pack up, I won't lie, I'm so glad she's gone, people had been mixing us up for years!"

I had completely forgotten that Gilliams was also a nurse, but I took this opportunity to ask about convictions that I couldn't find online.

As the women in the chow hall line passed through, one by one, if she knew what they were convicted of, she told me.

"You see that one at the first table with the two ponytails?"

"Yeah" I said, trying not to look directly at the one with the two ponytails.

"She killed her parents, decapitated them and then switched the heads. Had them officers all confused, momma's head on daddy's body and daddy's head on the body wearing a nightgown. She the one that called the cops because they started stinking, when the cops came in, crazy bitch was sitting in the kitchen eating a sandwich and they arrested her"

I didn't flinch.

"You see that one that just walked in?"

THE BLACKEST BLUE

"With the green jacket on?

"Yep", acting like I was reading something on my clipboard.

"She took the charge for her man in a drug raid, told the cops everything was hers. When the judge told her, I know that these drugs are not yours, this would be his third strike and you have no criminal history, so if you take the charge, be sure this is what you want to do. She took the charges, and the judge sentenced her to 60 years! Her man lied to her and told her that this was her first offense and that the judge was just trying to scare her into becoming a snitch, that was my first time hearing the term "You play stupid games; you win stupid prizes."

"What about this one in front of the line getting the green beans?" I questioned.

"Aww man, that's Davenport her story is messed up, her husband was a drunk and had like 3 DUI's, she kept telling him to stop drinking and driving or he's going to kill somebody, but instead of letting their twins catch the bus after school, he went and picked them up and drove with the kids in the car anyway, out of defiance."

"I don't understand" I said.

Chapter 15
Poker Face

"Yeah, well he killed somebody alright, he was drunk as a skunk and picked up their twins from high school, crashed into an 18-wheeler and both of the boys died...but his ass lived!"

"So then why is SHE in prison?"

"Oh, cuz she killed that motherfucker right after her boy's funeral, that's why!"

I held it together... I won the poker game! Deep down inside I wanted to yell "Get the fuck outta here!" But I just nodded my head and stayed quiet.

I was feeling good and confident as if I had just been initiated into a secret society. I passed the test and from what I understood from Sergeant Tuggle and Offender Gilliams, you really are not ready to hear these stories about people until you've been doing this for a few years, and now I see why.

I used my key to get in the ODR to do my daily inventory of which hot and cold food Offender McClellan was running low on.

She was in there alone, cleaning off the grill and in her own world. One more story won't hurt, right? I'm on a roll, I'm the poker face champ, I convinced myself. Inventory was complete, and I tried my hand at another game of poker.

"Hey McClellan, how much more time you got left on your sentence? I figured that was my subtle way of asking about her case.

She said, *"Oh, I got a ways to go, I've only done 7 on a 80."*

"80 years!!? What are you in here for? I questioned.

"You sure you wanna know?" she asked as she looked me dead in my eyes.

"I asked, didn't I?" Realizing I probably just wrote a check that my ass can't cash.

"Ok, I'll tell you, I guess you can handle it by now" she reasoned with herself.

I damn near wanted to say never mind, because in that moment it was crystal clear to me that **none** of the women on the Mountain View Unit were there for jay walking.

I was surrounded by the worst of the worst according to every Texas jury that ever made a unanimous decision.

Here I was, each time I heard someone's story, thinking if I was a juror, would I have convicted this person or that person?

"Well, McClellan said as she put the soapy cleaning rag in the square red bucket and sat down.

"I was with a man for about 3 years, he had a 1-year-old son when we met, the mom was on drugs and just left him with the baby not long after she had him. I had grown to love them both ...but me and Cody just wasn't getting along after a while. Nothing major happened, he just got colder and colder and froze me out. One day he called and invited me back over to his place, I was staying with my sister until I found my own apartment. We had only been broken up; I would say about 2 months at this point. He told me that Chase missed me, and could I come and spend some time with him. I won't lie... she continued, as she drifted off in her

131

thoughts as she told her story. It was bittersweet, I was hoping that Cody missed me too, because I missed our little family. It felt like old times, well to me anyway. As I watched her smile, thinking of the memory as she looked at the ceiling.

Then her smile disappeared, and she said, "It was very clear from the moment he saw me; he didn't miss me at all."

He even stepped out for a little bit while I was there, and I didn't think anything of it. He came back about 30 minutes later, went straight in his bedroom and I left. The next week, he asked if I would come by and spend time with Chase again, only this time when I got there, he was dressed up. Wranglers, button up shirt, cowboy hat and boots, big belt buckle, reminded me of how he used to dress when we first started dating. I thought to myself... Hmmm, he looks like he's going on a date or something...Is he trying to forget about me? Wait a damn minute...did I just go from the girlfriend to the fucking babysitter in a month? He walked out the door almost immediately after I got there, and I smelled his cologne lingering long after he got in his pick-up truck and pulled off.

Now I am church mouse quiet, as I watch her re-live the events and go back in time.

THE BLACKEST BLUE

"Officer, I just kept saying to myself over and over, he's trying to forget about me." He came back hours later, by then I had fed Chase, bathed him and put him to bed. I didn't say a word when he came in, I didn't have to, he was cold and standoffish. He thanked me for coming by and held the door open as a sign that I can leave now. I knew that if he asked me over there again, I would know for sure that he was not only dating someone new, but there was also no chance of us getting back together and to go on these dates, he was using me as a babysitter in the process.

Cody didn't even wait another week, the next damn day, he called me over again. Yep, Saturday night, I remember it like it was yesterday and yep, he was dressed up again. I said, "Are you dating someone already?" I wish I had held that question in, but I just wanted to know. He said, "What's it to you?" I said, "My gosh Cody... we just broke up, it's like you're trying to forget about me and move on!" He laughed a laugh that I can still hear to this day and said,

" Katherine, I forgot about us a long time ago, we're just friends."

And slammed the door as he walked out. I looked around at the place that I had called home a few weeks ago and wondered "how did we become just friends?" I nodded my head as the tears fell from my eyes and I said quietly to myself *"He's trying to forget me; we'll see about that just friends' shit." I went in the bedroom where Chase was playing with his train set and tapped his shoulder, I said,*

"Tag! You're it, Chase! "

And I ran into the living room. He scrambled to his little feet to join me in a game familiar to him and found me behind the sofa, and he said,

"Tag! You're it, Kathy!"

He hit my leg, giggled and ran off as fast as his little legs could go... I let him get near the kitchen before I tagged him again and ran behind the recliner, just as he got close to me, I stood up and blew his head off with Cody's shotgun!!

And I know, I know what you're going to ask me, "If I could go back in time and do it all over again would I?

Yep! His daddy was trying to forget about me...I bet he'll never forget me now!" she said with the amount of excitement that you find in prize winners.

"I know that's right! He sure won't forget about you!" I said, just as calm as I could muster.

As if I was co-signing this crazy shit.

THE BLACKEST BLUE

Man oh man!!!!!!!!!!!! I couldn't get my key in that lock fast enough and get my ass out of the ODR!

She just went right back to cleaning the grill like she had not just told me that crazy ass horror story! An officer walked in the ODR on their break, McClellan didn't miss a beat, she smiled and said, "What can I fix for you to eat?" Right back in character without a care in the world. I played it cool, but once I was on the other side of that door, I said, *"Lord have mercy!"* under my breath. I had lost my appetite and realized maybe I was not as ready as I thought, nope, nope, nope! I bet I didn't ask another soul about their story that day...I didn't want to play poker no more!

I had a few days off and when I returned, Major Fisher was in the kitchen, doing rounds and getting to know the staff. We had not had a Major on the unit since Major Kline was walked off for having sex with his trustee. She outsmarted the 22-year veteran. She literally *"Monica Lewinskied"* him. When he stopped bringing in the contraband she requested, she spit his DNA into a handkerchief and buried it under a flowerpot on the unit under the soil.

I don't even know how she got in contact with the FBI, but she knew somebody that knew somebody. The unit was locked down as the agents came on the unit and went directly to the exact flowerpot, removed the handkerchief and bagged it for evidence. Nobody, not the Warden, not even Major Kline himself was aware of what was going on.

A few weeks later, his morning meeting was interrupted, and he was placed in handcuffs in front of his staff. Major Kline was put in the back of a squad car, booked and processed on a number of charges.

How do you even explain how your semen and an offender's saliva is mixed together in a handkerchief...how do you tell this to your wife?! Retirement, gone! Everything he worked so hard for, out the window!

All because he wouldn't continue to sneak in more make-up but wanted to continue having her perform sexual favors. Idiot!

Chapter 16

Sign Right Here and Right Here Too

N ow remember, I told you, the first time I got my heart broken, was by my **own.** Let me tell you that I felt like I was under attack, back-to-back to back. Each time, the pain was deeper because the officer looked like me, black! Major Fisher was by definition what you would consider mulatto… half black and half white. He definitely identified with the black side of his family. He was a tall but slim brother and made sure you knew he was from Chicago. With a gold tooth on the side, red hair and freckles, he confused the hell out of most black people, but he

137

couldn't pass for white either. Especially with his hood personality. The fact that he loved to give everybody a dap instead of a handshake was odd for a man in his position, but that was how he greeted everyone, and I do mean everyone. He was a very, very light skinned African American man, in his mid to late 30's, his hair texture also gave him away but if he didn't try so hard to prove to black people that he was black, you would at least wonder for a second, and I do mean a second. It was easy to tell by his swag that he was a brother, he made sure it was known by the way he walked and talked. I thought it was odd how he greeted us and how much slang he used just to prove a point. I didn't judge his overacting of a black man. In hindsight, he reminded me of a male in drag, overaccentuating everything deliberately. Personally, I thought he was cool and down to earth. That was all I thought of him. I didn't know him well enough to like him or dislike him.

As soon as he walked into the kitchen office, offender James, the kitchen secretary said,

"Hey Major, you didn't call out E-Dorm again today, did you?"

He laughed and said "No, not today." As he turned a little red from embarrassment.

I said, *"E-Dorm?" That dorm has been closed for over 10 years since the last execution before Franny Newt, what do you mean call them out?"*

I was really asking offender James, but he answered me and said,

"Yeah, I'm still learning the unit, I called the dorms out for chow 1 by 1 over the radio yesterday, but when I got to E-Dorm, I called 3 times, and nobody answered.

I said, *"Well Sir that's because E-Dorm is the old Death Row housing, they didn't answer because all of those people are dead!"*

We all busted out laughing. He nodded and said,

"Yeah, I know, they sent somebody over to the chow hall to let me know I was calling out an empty dorm, I guess they didn't want to make me look dumb over the radio."

He shook his head as he laughed at himself and walked out the door.

About an hour later, the phone rung and Captain Hamlin said to me,

"The Major wants to see you in his office."

Clearly, I'm walking up there thinking he needed me to do something, because the unit was short staffed. I walked in his office, ready to give him the usual dap greeting, but his face looked nothing like the one I saw earlier. I thought to myself "oh shit", withdrew my fist, and sat down. Clearly, he was in his "professional mode", I just didn't get the memo.

I asked,

" Sir, you wanted to see me. Is everything ok?"

He got up and closed the door and with the most serious face, I had ever seen on him since he started working here about 2 months ago, he said,

"No, everything is not ok, what you did back there was completely unprofessional! I could see if you wanted to clown with me off to the side, but you embarrassed me in front of an offender!"

I was shocked at the way he processed that entire situation.

"Sir, I didn't even know you called out E-Dorm. I was off yesterday, Offender James mentioned it to you, and you joked about it, how am I the one being unprofessional? Forgive me, if you feel I embarrassed you, but I promise, that was not my intentions at all."

He could give two shits about my attempt at logic or my apology. He kept on talking like I didn't say a word 5 seconds ago.

" *This* *is* *your* *verbal* *warning,* *conduct* *yourself* *professionally at all times in front of these offenders, are we* *clear?"*

I said, *"Yes Sir."* But my eyes were saying, "What the fuck just happened here?"

"You're excused." He said, with a tone that really sounded like *"Get the hell out of my office!"*

I quietly opened the door and left his office. I could literally feel my heart break. The fact that he was black felt like a dagger in my heart…seriously. I was confused and annoyed at the same time because, he knew that I didn't initiate that conversation, I really felt like he should have just checked Offender James on the spot. Especially if he felt like this would have been embarrassing to him, instead of laughing and playing along. I went back to work and finished my day.

It really bothered me how I watched a black man gain power and authority, lose his sense of humor in the process. The next day when I came in, I was refreshed and ready to put the past behind me. But the moment that I opened the kitchen office door, Captain Hamlin said,

THE BLACKEST BLUE

"The Major wants to see you in his office again."

I'm thinking, *"What the fuck did I do now?"*

I didn't even tell a soul what happened yesterday when I came back from his office, so I knew it couldn't be anything dealing with that.

My balloon of energy was deflated as I took that long walk up to the Administration Offices. *"What could he possibly want with me?"* I thought. When I got to his office, the door was closed, I knocked and as he waved me in and motioned for me to close the door. I immediately noticed a piece of paper on his desk with my name on it when I looked down.

I said,

"Sir, you wanted to see me again?"

He said, *"Absolutely! What you did yesterday just didn't sit well with me and I decided to write you up for unprofessional conduct."*

My eyebrows raised as I said,

"Write me up? But Sir, yesterday you said that you were giving me a verbal warning, what happened to that?"

And as cold as a January in New York he said, *"Yeah, well I changed my mind."*

I didn't even know if he could or couldn't do that, what I did know was that I was furious. He said, *"Sign right here."* as he pointed to the X on the bottom of the paper. *"And here too"*, as he pointed to another X.

I asked, "So is this going to go in my permanent file?"

"It sure is!" He said, with the cockiness of "who's laughing now?"

He was pissed, even more today than he was yesterday.

I said, "Oh wow" as I read how he twisted the events on the disciplinary document about my role in yesterday's situation. He knew that he had just assassinated my career with that write up, and all he did was hand me his gold pen to sign it with.

He was one lie away from being able to accuse me of insubordination. I knew that it would be pointless to talk to the Sergeant and Lieutenant on duty, he outranked everyone on the unit other than the Warden and the Assistant Warden. I doubted if anyone would commit career suicide on my behalf, especially once they got to see just how dishonest he could be when describing an incident.

I signed the write up, put my copy in my pocket and walked out.

I was beyond angry; I was fucking furious! Not just at how he turned that entire situation around but at his deliberate choice to change the verbal warning to an official write up after the fact. Like, who does this?

I had not received a write-up or even a warning at all in the 4 years that I had been working on the unit.

For my first one to be by a Major, it held a lot of weight, and he knew that. There's no way he didn't!

He knew that any attempt for me to be promoted to Sergeant would not happen with a write up of unprofessional conduct in my file, especially a write up coming from the rank of a Major. He knew that as a black woman in law enforcement, it was harder for us to move up being a double minority. He knew that he was fucking me over and he didn't give a shit.

I went back into the kitchen office and Offender James kept watching me, looking for a signal to see if everything was ok. I just sat there and shook my head. She said, "I'm so sorry." I didn't respond, I didn't need to. I continued sitting there, pretty much checked out. I didn't even have to tell her that things didn't go well, she knew.

It had to have been a day or two after the incident with the Major when I was picking up my little girl up from elementary school. I saw an officer in a completely different uniform than that washed out gray and blue we wear at TDCJ. Ours was handmade by offenders and most of the time the blue stripe going down the side of the leg was crooked, or one sleeve was longer than the other. You just keep changing them out until you find a decent complete uniforms.

Well anyway, the uniform I saw was a tan collared shirt and blue pants, with SHERIFF patches sewn on, she had her pants tucked in her combat boots and I liked the way the uniform looked. Like a bad ass!

I introduced myself and inquired about where she worked. Officer Bullock said that she worked at the Williamson County Sheriff's Office in Georgetown Texas. For a million dollars, I couldn't tell you where Georgetown Texas was, but for free, I vowed I would find it! I could tell that my time on Mountain View was going to come to an abrupt end, especially after the way the new Major conducted business. I just needed to make sure I had a backup plan, just in case this was not the last of his Jeckel and Hyde bullshit.

Chapter 17

The Trouble Has Doubled

The officer told me how much Williamson County made, the hours they worked and the difference between a street deputy and a jail deputy. I could become a court Bailiff or a transportation deputy for extraditions. Then she said if I wanted her to bring me an application, she would bring it up to the school the next day. I was like, wow they don't even have positions like that at the prison and then it dawned on me why so many people confuse jails and prisons, because they are **NOT** the same at all. Officer Bullock brought the packet to me the next day. I didn't know the application would be 35 pages long though. I said, *"THIS is an application, just to be a Corrections Officer?"*

She laughed and said, *"Yes Ma'am, we're nothing like TDCJ, we do an extensive background check, credit score check, we even do a home visits before you get hired on."*

"Wow, ok. When do you need this back by?"

I asked as I held up the hiring packet. *"Whenever you get done with it, just bring it back to me and I'll turn it in for you."*

We exchanged phone numbers; I thanked her and went home.

I completed the hiring packet for Williamson County that same week. My heart wasn't in it at TDCJ anymore, there was no way that I could act like nothing happened, I was done. Each shift in the kitchen had two supervisors, three officers on each shift and then we had a kitchen captain over all of us.

Depending on the supervisor rotation, I worked with Mrs. Parker or Mr. Jefferson the most. Both of them were black, and Ms. Vogle was a short-tempered German woman on first shift. I was on the second shift. Ms. Vogle was an overseer, the iron fist, harsh type. The others were laid back. Mrs. Parker, a heavy-set Puerto Rican and black woman who wanted the world to know that she was married to a black man. Was also from New York, the Bronx, and we hit it off from day one. But shortly after my write up, it just seemed like, shit kept going downhill.

I waited for Williamson County to call me, but they didn't. I left about 9 messages on their training department's voicemail for 2 months, one a week and still nothing. I asked Officer Bullock every time that I saw her at the school, but she worked nights, so she rarely saw the training officers.

One afternoon, Mrs. Parker said,

"Hey, switch keys with me, I need you to do a dumpster run."

Basically, that meant getting about six offenders and collecting trash from all over the unit, from the kitchen and the kitchen's back dock, then taking all of that trash to the dumpster. It takes a while to complete, but we do it every day just usually at the end of the shift. I thought the request was odd at this time of day, but I just grabbed a crew and got it done. No questions asked.

Here is where I fucked up.

From my first day in the kitchen, Captain Hamlin told me, "*If you get keys or switch keys, sign out the keys in the logbook. Don't just do it and not document it.*"

We went all day with me having keys that I didn't sign out and when it was time to leave for the day, the set that I had given her was nowhere to be found...and guess who those keys were assigned to? My dumb ass, without documentation! Now, you can't get convicted criminals to assist you with looking for keys, so after the offenders were strip searched as they normally are daily, before being sent back to their perspective dorms, Mrs. Parker, Ms. Washington and I checked the kitchen for the missing keys. Mrs. Parker checked the key and utensil closet. She didn't find the keys.

Ms. Washington and I checked the office. No keys. We looked everywhere, even places I knew I didn't go, still nothing. She notified the on-shift Sergeant and Lieutenant and although I had keys, they were not the ones signed out to me. They sent a few officers over to assist us in the search as Mrs. Parker swore to God and country that she gave me the keys back, but she did not! We looked by the dumpsters and still nothing. I was annoyed at the fact that we were looking in places that I knew I didn't lose the keys because I didn't have them since I put them in her hands.

THE BLACKEST BLUE

Captain Hamlin was called at home, and it was becoming a big deal. The part that got me was, they were signed out to me, but it was the set that I traded with Mrs. Parker, my supervisor.

Sergeant Hicks said,

" Ok, walk me through it, step by step, what happened when you first came in to work?

And here I am, doing a motherfucking reenactment... like I lost a set of keys when I didn't! I go to the front door and walk in as everyone is watching, the only thing missing is the popcorn.

"Ok, and then what do you do next?" He asked.

"I go in here" I pointed to the key and utensil closet.

"But someone would have to unlock the door for me from the previous shift and when we take the keys out of the locked cage, two officers have to sign them out, the person that opened the door for me and then I sign too."

He turned and said, *"Mrs. Parker, so where do you turn in your keys after you guys' lock everything up? "At the front gate",* she said.

But your keys are still on you now, correct? May I see them?

THE BLACKEST BLUE

Sergeant Hicks opened the door to the key closet and then opened the cage door where keys are hung on a shadow board and said," *Which keys are you missing?* I said, *"Apparently the ones I signed out, key # 93, but I didn't have them, she did."* He took the supervisor's indoor keys off the hook on the shadow board and there was key set #93, behind hers!

"She said," *I swear I looked in there."*

I just rolled my eyes and didn't say a word. I can't wait to see how this plays out in the morning to Captain Hamlin. I thought.

I could hear the group of officer's mumble under their breath about how much of a waste of time this was.

Not only did she not apologize, when I came in the next day, there was a write-up waiting for me in the office. SHE was writing me up for not logging in the book that I had switched keys. I said,

"Are you joking? YOU had my keys!"

She said," *Major Fisher wrote me up and instructed me to write you up for not documenting that you had a different set of keys, I signed mine, so sign yours and let's move on."*

The audacity!

THE BLACKEST BLUE

I wanted to say, *"Bitch fuck you!"*

I just signed near the first and second X and left the office. I signed the write up because I honestly didn't log that I had switched the keys. I couldn't prove what was said, but they could prove what wasn't written down. That was on me.

I had enough of TDCJ and these write ups at this point. The way things go around here. Dirty, Dirty!

I just didn't understand why Mrs. Parker didn't tell the truth. Why did she let everyone believe that I had made the mistake of misplacing the damn keys? To top it off, she even looked in that same closet and swore on everything but a stack of bibles that the keys were not in there. That's what really had me pissed off. Like I really started to feel like everything was a set up from the moment she switched keys with me. I'm also trying to wrap my head around this new write up. As I sat in my car on my break, I thought, *"What is the deal with Major Fisher and why is he dead set on stacking the deck against me?*

But before I could come up with answers to any of those questions, I needed to call Gwen and catch her up on this bullshit. She's been working for TDCJ for years and I needed her guidance. I told her how our new Major was on my ass. She asked, *"Major Fisher? Light skinned brother, like reallll light, motherfucker remind me of Kid from Kid and Play without the flat top!"*

I died laughing and said, "Yep! That's exactly who he looks like, that motherfucker is fucking with me like I remind him of an ex-girlfriend or something."

Gwen was pissed about that verbal warning that he changed his mind on, and she said, *"He's not even supposed to keep bringing you in his office without another supervisor being present, what if you say he said or did something sexual to you, damn he's not even covering his own ass, that's crazy. But girl, don't be nobody's fool, don't let him just do whatever the fuck he want to do. Ask questions but stay respectful because he is definitely trying to stack the deck on you!"*

As she's talking, I see that I had received a text from Officer Bullock, *"Someone from Williamson County should be in contact with you today."* She had emailed the training Sergeant, and they responded to her email. "Thank God" was my reply, and I went back inside smiling as if I didn't feel that sting of betrayal.

"Fuck you, you fat white bitch!" "I'm not listening to shit you tell me, you racist bitch, fat stink hoe ass bitch!"

Chapter 18

The Switch

I could hear the screaming coming from the doorway as my kitchen crew pushed the food cart into the Administrative Segregation building. I worked in Ad Seg plenty of times and I knew that voice like I knew my own. Shakeia McCrae was not a troublesome offender, she spent most of her time singing and writing songs, so to hear her yelling like that was not normally how I remembered her, and she was definitely not disrespectful to officers. I asked, "Is that McCrae in there yelling like that?"

Officer Holland just rolled her eyes and said, *"Yep".*

She pretended like she didn't care, but her face was as red as a tomato. She definitely cared and was mad too. Now here I go, trying to fix shit so that she didn't punish McCrae later for embarrassing her. I know how some officers can be when they get mad. I said, "Do *you want me to talk to her, she's usually not like this."*

She said, *"You're not going to be able to calm her down, I have been every fat white, fat stinky coochie bitch she can think of for the last 3 hours because I don't jump when she needs something, hell she's not going anywhere for another 40 years, she can wait!"*

I said, *"Stand at the door with my crew and I'll try to calm her down."*

She stepped aside and said,*" Good luck!"*

"McCrae!!" I yelled as I turned the corner.

"Fuck you cracker bitch, I bet your husband hate you, fucking stink coochie bitch!!"

I said, *"Shakeia McCrae! You know better!"*

by this time, I am standing directly in front of her cell.

THE BLACKEST BLUE

She said *"Heyyyyy!!! You're not Officer Holland, why you don't work in here with us anymore, we miss you, we need more black officers in here?"*

I said, *"McCrae, I get it, but you can't do that...you can't be disrespectful, she's going to write you up, I just need you to cut it out!"*

"Ma'am, all I did was ask her for toilet tissue and pads? But she's a racist, she gives the white girls their shit when they ask for it, but when i asked, she sat my roll of tissue on her desk so that I can see it, but she won't give it to me, I can't get it myself locked in this fucking cage all day, but now that I'm calling her names, she saying shit like "You ain't going nowhere, I'll give it to you in a minute."

I just shook my head as I listened to her tell me how Officer Holland does some questionable shit. I grabbed the roll of toilet tissue and a few pads from the pack and gave it to Offender McCrae.

"Now be respectful, your mother raised you better than that! Stop all of that yelling, I could hear you from outside." I warned her.

I didn't know McCrae's mother, but I remember the stories she used to tell me about the relationship she had with her mom and her little sister Nicky. I worked where McCrae was housed for 6 months straight before going into the kitchen. She told me so much about her family, and I knew what it would take to calm her down. To de-escalate the situation, I used that information, and it worked like a charm.

"Yes, Ma'am, you're right my momma raised me right, I'll chill out, but I'm only doing this for you, not that fat white, stink coochie, racist bitch!" All of the convicts in the nearby cells laughed.

I just gave her the "Now what did I just tell you?" look. McCrae thanked me for the supplies and chilled out like she said she would. And just like that, the situation was over. Or at least that was what I had hoped to accomplish. I told Officer Holland that she would behave, I should have known something was up when she didn't say *"thank you"*.

By the time we finished taking the food carts to the Death Row unit and all three Cell Blocks, I was called up to the office by Major Fisher, AGAIN! Yeah, you guessed it, my attempts to de-escalate the situation turned into another fucking write up!

Apparently, Officer Holland, didn't like the fact that I came into her post and *"took over"* by giving an offender the feminine hygiene items that she requested and waited over an hour for. From what I read, as I glanced down at the paper on his desk, Officer Holland was going to give McCrae the pads and tissue herself, whenever she got around to it. Somehow, I managed to undermine her authority. As if she didn't step aside at the door and wish me luck on calming McCrae down.

I was also written up for unprofessional conduct, I was told that calling an offender by their first name was unprofessional. Now why in the world would Officer Holland switch up on me like that, when all I did was calm McCrae down and get her to stop being disrespectful towards her. I thought I was helping!!

Holland's actions let me know that there was validity to the fact that she was a racist. She didn't think I could get McCrae to calm down and then when I did, it became a problem, for me and for McCrae, because she was written up for a laundry list of violations.

I had had it with Major Fisher. I said,

"Sir, this is the second time I have been written up by you and you didn't ask me my side of the story. Whatever Officer Holland told you is her version of the story. It's like I'm guilty until proven guilty."

He said, *"Did you call an offender by her first name?"* I just stared at him, because I did call her by her first name...but this was bullshit, and he knew it.

He said, "Did you give an offender feminine supplies when that wasn't your assigned duty post?"

I shook my head at how this entire situation changed up in a matter of minutes.

"I thought I was helping Officer Holland, and for whatever reason she complained, there are sergeants, lieutenants and captains on duty today. Why is everything handled at your level when it comes to me, like it's personal?"

This bastard literally took that golden pen from his pocket while I was talking and handed it out towards me, like just sign near the X and fuck whatever I had to say because it didn't matter.

Well, I guess that meant that two of us didn't give a shit that day because not only was he on my ass again like it was personal, but once again, I was in his office with the door closed and no other supervisor. He needed a taste of his own medicine. I refused to sign the write up, I left his hand hanging with that gold pen in it. I was done playing games with his arrogant ass.

THE BLACKEST BLUE

Still holding that gold pen out like he was frozen in time, Major Fisher said, "If you refuse to sign this disciplinary form, I will take it to the Warden and see if I can place you on Administrative Leave."

I looked at him…and it felt like slow motion when I looked at that fancy ass pen in his hand. I looked down at the paper on his desk with the lies written on it, stood up and walked right out of his office.

Fuck him!!!

THE BLACKEST BLUE

It was like he was power tripping and getting off doing this to me. I felt like whatever the consequences will be, I'll take them up with the Warden. I knew I would be on the Major's shit list, so I stopped by the Warden's office and made an appointment with her secretary to tell her my side. This one-sided dance with the devil had gone on long enough. The warden was a respected and fair black woman. At this rate, I would take a fair alien from Mars because everyone seemed so unfair here and race had nothing to do with it. I felt like Warden Chasen needed to know what was happening on her unit. I called the kitchen and told Captain Hamlin that I needed to go back to my car for a minute. He probably could tell from my tone that I was upset.

I really needed a minute to myself to gather my composure, how do you even describe being mistreated by your own? Let down, confused and angry I didn't know how much more of this black-on-black crime I could take.

I wasn't in my car for 5 minutes when my cellphone started ringing from a number I didn't recognize.

"Hello?"

"Good afternoon, this is Sergeant Winfree from the Williamson County Sheriff's Office. Sorry for the delay, we

had some major changes in the training department, and I see that you have left multiple messages and even had Officer Bullock email me. Are you available tomorrow for testing? There's a written test and then a physical agility test."

"Oh Yes! Thank you for calling me, your timing is perfect. I'm off for the next 3 days. I do have a question though, provided that I pass everything, how fast can we complete the process for me to get hired on?"

"To be totally honest, I feel bad that it took us almost 3 months to get back to you. We had some ummm, personnel changes in the training department, so I definitely owe you one, I'll make a deal with you, if you pass everything, I will fast track your hiring process myself. You will have to take your psych evaluation on Thursday. They only do those evaluations on Thursdays. I can speed up your background and I would say, I could get you hired within 2-3 weeks if all goes well, just do your best and I got it on my end."

"That's music to my ears, you have a deal and thank you Sergeant Winfree!"

"No, thank you! For your patience." He said as he ended the call.

THE BLACKEST BLUE

Sergeant Winfree gave me hope, for real. He also sounded like a man of his word, so I was ready to leave this place and give Wilco a shot.

Chapter 19

Rights and Hostages

Not just because Major Fisher was going out of his way to commit career homicide, but we were only getting paid once a month, you work in the elements, heavy rain, the bitter cold, 105-degree Texas summer heat and they have this thing in Texas called "black ice". Now I had never heard of it, snow is snow and ice is ice in the Big Apple, but that black ice in Texas is a silent killer. It's basically after the temperature drop, that sheet of ice on the black top we walk or drive on...now you don't really see it, but I tell you what...when that car start sliding, or it get up under your feet as you walk, you'll feel it!! I would much rather work in an environment where people still have hope, the potential to get out of their situation or even found "not guilty".

I know that plenty of people confuse jails with prisons, but they are definitely not the same thing. In a county jail, you are not sentenced yet, you can have different classes of misdemeanors or different degrees of felonies.

In jail, inmates still have their constitutional rights, they can possibly have the case thrown out by the District Attorney before it ever gets anywhere near a jury, receive a bond and just go to court or trial from home, receive probation, placed on an ankle monitor and never be sentenced to prison time.

In a prison, a person had to have plead guilty or been found guilty, by a judge or a jury. Convicted and sentenced to a certain number of years and in some states, sentenced to death, if you are blessed enough to be released early, you will be on parole for some time, however, when you are in prison, you no longer have rights. If you get written up in prison, you could go months without recreation. The same thing that is a constitutional right in one place is a "yeah right" in another.

Don't believe the myth that you still have "some" rights...sure ok. Some....rhymes with none. Having a family member call up to the jail to ask questions about why an inmate was written up or why didn't an inmate receive their commissary would NEVER in a million years happen once they are sentenced to prison. All of that babying bullshit would fly out the window instantly. But I digress.

I caught myself smiling as I was walking back to the front gate, and quickly wiped that shit off. Had to switch back to my Resting Bitch Face, which I apply daily, right after I put on my eyeliner. It's almost like, being happy or making an accomplishment is a sin in a place like this. Don't buy a car, a house, get married or have a baby...first of all, all of your business will spread all over the unit faster than gossip can travel on a reality TV show. The sad part is, the officers tell your business to another officer loud enough for an offender to hear, or the worst of the worst case is when an officer tells an offender your business directly. That shit will piss you off, imagine being on vacation for a week and on your first day back to work, you have offenders asking you "So, how was Jamaica?" You won't even blink, you'll look them dead in their eyes and have the sharp wit to say,

"I wouldn't know, how was it when you went?"

THE BLACKEST BLUE

As soon as the gate guard buzzed me in, I could hear the commotion over the radio and the officers running from every direction. I said to the officer in the guard shack, "What the heck happened now?" She said, "You better hurry, we have a hostage situation!" This was a first for me. I dealt with fights and several escapes in the juvenile detention facility, but how is this even possible on the unit?

I run in the direction everyone else is running in and I see a group of offenders running in the direction of the rec yard, being escorted by two officers.

The high-ranking supervisors off to the side trying to come up with a strategy while officers try to negotiate from the threshold.

Sergeant Price is waving me over and asking me if I have a rapport with offender Best?

Out of all of the prisoners on the unit, she was the one that you would pray took her medication every day, because offender Annette Best off of Thorazine, was not someone that anyone ever wanted to deal with! Missing a few screws was an understatement. I mean, her elevator went up, but the door didn't open! Best was a tall and stocky built black woman, that pretty much stayed to herself. Unless you had x-ray vision and could see her imaginary friends, she really didn't talk to anyone else but them.

Apparently, she had a headache and was taking a nap prior to this incident. Offender Best asked Officer Green to stop the distracting noise from her keys as they were crashing into her thighs when the officer walked back and forth.

The sway of her hips made the keys hit the front and side of her thigh and gave away her location with every movement she made, loudly. Officer Green didn't even acknowledge the request, if you ask the other offenders, after Best made the request, the keys seemed to make even more noise, like she was deliberately being louder. Best knew that this white officer was blowing her off. Without her meds and a headache, she took that as sign of disrespect, especially because the sound woke her up and she already asked nicely twice. When Officer Green entered the bunk area to do her next round of visuals, her keys were snatched so hard away from her body that Offender Best was able to rip the beltloop on the uniform pants completely off! She backed the officer into a corner, with rage in her eyes. Unfortunately, in the same corner where another offender was sweeping, she took the broom from that offender and grabbed the both of them. Offender Annette Best had snapped!

THE BLACKEST BLUE

Officer Green was able to hit her panic button before things went from bad to worse.

As I looked in the doorway. I see that Best had the broomstick across Officer Green's throat with her right hand, and she had the offender that was sweeping, in a headlock with her left arm.

As soon as she sees me and Sergeant Price, she said, "And don't y'all bring y'all black asses in here, I don't want to hurt nobody, but I will!!" At this point, I'm coughing my ass off from the pepper spray smoke. Clearly, I can see there are 4 empty pepper spray cans laying on the floor in the dorm. The spray has zero effect on Best, one of the cons of being on Thorazine, your senses are distorted. She could barely smell anything, but she could hear an ant run over a Q-tip. Once the medication is taken, we would watch them walk super-duper slowly and sway from side to side; that walk is known to everyone as "The Thorazine Shuffle". They really should have named it "The Comatose Two-Step" because they are barely awake walking back to the dorms.

At this point, Officer Green and the offender that had been taken hostage were both coughing uncontrollably and visibly crying.

I watched with my eyes without turning my head to see Officer Booker go around the back of the building. I could see him through the windows behind offender Best. I already knew he was going to sneak in through the fire door. Our job was to keep her distracted and facing us, knowing that the fire door didn't alarm or alert. The offender she held hostage began gagging so hard it sounded like she would throw up and Best just simply let her go...just like that, she released the headlock.

We waved the newly released hostage over to us, but she was so disoriented from the amount of smoke and the level of her own panic that she just froze in place. It was like instinct; Sergeant Price and I both ran in just past the threshold and pulled her out. We didn't even discuss doing that, but our actions caused offender Best to stand up from the officer's chair and glare at us. She applied more pressure with the broomstick right up under Officer Green's throat, using both hands this time. Sergeant Booker was a very large man, he stood about 6'8 and no less than 365 pounds. Not a sound came from the fire door as he crept through undetected. He was in stealth mode as the negotiations continued but Best was not in her right mind, period. Talking to her was like talking to a caged animal.

THE BLACKEST BLUE

Reasoning and rationale were like foreign languages, and she just had no interest in communicating with anyone.

She had no demands, nothing that we offered made sense to her. She said, "I don't want anything from y'all! All I wanted was for this bitch to stop making so much motherfucking noise with them goddamn keys when she walks by my bed...that's all I want!" By then Officer Booker knocked her to the ground and it was hammer time!

She was laid out cold when Mr. Fleming gave her a shot in her arm of that "liquid night night".

She had refused this same medication all week and now she's in a mountain of trouble. The offenders were removed from the rec yard and allowed back in the dorm after it was cleaned, decontaminated and aired out.

And just like that, the policy was changed the next day. Every supervisor had to read it to their subordinate, and we all had to initial the document to say that we were aware of it. In other words, if you fuck up and let those keys clank and rattle like they belonged to a janitor, your ass was going to get written up by the warden herself, period!

THE BLACKEST BLUE

*"Effective immediately, **ALL** keys, whether personal or professional, will be placed in a pants or shirt pocket to reduce noise and distractions."*

Warden Chasen

Once the warden signed it herself through DocuSign. We all thought, *"Well damn, that was quick!"*

Chapter 20

Forensic Leftovers

"*L*ive, breathing body headcounts." I could hear them telling us this in my sleep! Every Sergeant and Lieutenant drilled this in our heads, every single day in briefing. We heard it so much that if you messed up headcount, it was going to be a big deal. If headcount was not conducted and cleared within one hour, the phones would start ringing and then an order from up high would demand that we shut the entire facility down. As long as you work in Corrections, a person under a blanket, not visible to you...is what we call a dead body count. If you can't see them breathing or talking, how can you account for signs of life if you had to swear to it under oath? You can't! So, on your watch, you'd better do every headcount by the standard! Or don't... and deal with the consequences of not doing your job. Old Lady Durham was not a joy to deal with, mostly out of fear than anything. She would only speak to certain people, whether it was an offender or an officer. By certain people, I mean black people. She was mean as shit to white people. I believe age played a part. At 85 years old, she watched so many of her loved ones over the years, get falsely accused, incarcerated and even lynched just for being in the wrong place and in the wrong skin. I couldn't tell at first if she had dementia or if she was just demonic. Her conduct was explained to me by an offender as a warning. She's either going to like you or hate you, she does not have a middle or a gray area.

She told me to watch Durham's eyes and they will teach me everything I needed to know. My first encounter with her eyes spoke volumes, I was putting an offender in her place for trying to run shit. I said, *"Go back to your cell, you don't run shit but your mouth and that shower!"* When I told the control room to roll the door, I turned and was met with a pair of 85-year-old twinkling eyes and a grandmotherly face to match. *"It's about time somebody checked that cracker,*

Good morning, Officer, are you here all day?" "Yes, Ma'am I am, and good morning to you too." I didn't entertain her racist remark. Immediately, I was her favorite, maybe because she thought that I didn't like white people, but that wasn't the case. I will check your ass if you're black, white, Hispanic, Asian, old or young, period. I was THAT officer. I was told that Deanna Durham wasn't always like this, however she was 65 years old when she killed her entire family at the same time. The word "entire" in this situation, would also include two dogs.

Old Lady Durham talked to me for a long time, almost like she needed to tell her side of a story, after years of silence. A few years ago, she decided that Thanksgiving would be a good way to pay everyone back that had gone against her in a family issue involving property and money. Let her tell it, she was a good cook, even considered opening her own soul food restaurant one day. Her youngest daughter, Diane, was a flight attendant and a delay during the holidays saved her life. From the way it sounds, she will always believe in her heart that the delayed flight is why she's still alive, and from what I heard…she's right!. Had she made it home in time for dinner, she would have been deliberately poisoned along with everyone else. As each family member went around the table fixing their plates, they outwardly expressed what they were thankful for. Good energy surrounded the room and although the Dallas Cowboys were on the screen, the tv was turned down low.

Daryl Durham, her oldest son, lead the family in prayer, an amen in unison and just as she knew they would, everyone began eating at the exact same time. That was the family tradition. She knew the day that her parents' attorney read the will to everyone that this day would come, and it would come very soon. She knew to hold her anger in and try to reason with her loved. What was clearly a clerical error in the will, became an opportunity for greed to step in and for hatred to fester. Deanna Durham was her parents first born; she was the one who took care of her siblings while her parents built a fortune in their businesses. She was the one that took care of them after they got sick. Not her siblings, and not anyone else in the family, for that matter. Nana and Papa Durham were heavy smokers, mostly due to the stress of being wealthy and black in the south. You would think they would have less stress, but there was always an issue, that required money. They were both diagnosed with the big C in the same year.

Their love was like the movie "The Notebook" and without each other, they would pass away only 5 months apart.

THE BLACKEST BLUE

Everyone in the family was aware of how the Durham's handled business from the generations before them. It had always been known that Deanna would inherit the house and 100 acres of land. Her brothers would inherit the chain of $1.00 retail stores called *"One Acre"*, her parents called it that because, one acre, is how much land they started with. There were 24 stores in total, all over the south, their stores would be what we call "Dollar Tree" now. The Durhams made sure that nothing was to be sold to anyone outside of the bloodline and after Deanna passed, the next one in line was Dennis, her brother. Donnie would follow and the order would go just like that for the grandchildren as well. This was a foolproof system, to avoid chaos within the family while simultaneously allowing maturity to seep in before it's the next family members turn to take over.

However, someway, somehow, the clerk made a huge mistake and the "100 acres" and "One Acre" retail stores were transposed...leaving Deanna Durham with the house and ONE ACRE OF LAND! Instead of her family members informing the attorney that there was an obvious mistake, they shut their mouths and hoped that there was nothing that she could do about it. She tried to explain the family tradition and how things had been done in the family for years, but the documents with their parents' signatures was what was solid and legally binding. She caught herself using her outside voice and quickly realized that everyone in the room had selective amnesia. To include the family attorney. Dennis and Donnie Durham divided up the retail stores and the other 99 acres with their children, a few cousins and even sold some of the land. This was completely out of order and would have their ancestors turning in their graves if that was a thing. There were even some distant relatives that called to express their outrage at the deliberate disrespect of the Durham legacy. They meant well when they assured her that she could fight this in court and win. They also encouraged her to stay calm and let God handle the situation. But her younger siblings continued to ignore her calls and handwritten letters in an attempt to rectify the situation. They immediately began to build a mini mall, a car repair shop and a laundromat within a 1-mile radius of each other. They avoided the truth altogether and just simply didn't acknowledge shit. She tried to reason with them, collectively, and when that failed, she approached them individually. They continued to play possum. I was all ears as she relived this pain, she used her entire hour out in the dayroom to tell me why she was in prison in her elder years.

Inside she was furious, but that internal lava dying to erupt would have to wait a little while longer, she explained.

THE BLACKEST BLUE

Karma was served in a martini glass with ice and sugar around the rim one autumn afternoon.

She had hoped for a resolve, but the family attorney advised her that she shouldn't waste her time. His reward for that lie was two acres of land under an alias. As was the court clerk, she received one acre in compensation for the "clerical error" that could not be reversed. Since the will was read aloud shortly after both of her parents passing, everyone blamed their sudden bout with amnesia on the fact that they were grieving.

Deanna wasn't buying it and as the saying goes, *"What's done in the dark will come to light!"* One thing she knew about her family and their traditions. She would cook every holiday and they would eventually come around for her cooking. There was no doubt about that. October 12th, she got a call from her son Daryl who was suffering from the flu. With everyone else at work, he called Deanna and asked her to pick up his prescription and also if she could make her signature chicken noodle soup.

She loved her son and because he wasn't involved in that family mess, she had no problem taking care of him while he was ill. The medicine and the bowl of his momma's chicken noodle soup worked wonders. But unfortunately for him, as soon as he began to snore, the group text in his phone began to fire off in rapid session. In an attempt to quiet the chimes before they disturbed her ailing son, Deanna picked up the phone to turn off the ringer and there she could see countless messages exposing the fact that they were all in cahoots to steal the 99 acres and make it look like a mistake.

They were all involved, all of them, her brothers, the family members that called, and even her own children. She could literally feel her heart break.

Deanna had time to read all of their thoughts and feelings about her and even how they made jokes at her expense. *"She's cooking for us on Thanksgiving, talk about biting the hand that feeds you"* one of her niece's texts read.

"We should try to get her to cook for Christmas too." Her brother chimed in through text. The camera system in Daryl's house would pick up her voice as she said out loud, *"You motherfuckers won't live to see Christmas!"*

The camera also picked up on her putting his cell phone back on the living room table and walking out. They played the videos in court, she told me. She calmly and methodically made sure that she reached out to every family member in that group chat, making sure that she got everyone's RSVP for Thanksgiving.

Enticing them with an early Christmas gift if they would attend. Their greed alone, would be their demise.

As the high levels of cyanide laced food, in their favorite dishes began to take effect, one by one, they would all drop dead, some still with a fork in their hand. Twenty-three family members, twenty-five if you counted her brother's dogs.

The only one alive in the house was Deanna Durham, with a TV dinner rotating in the microwave and a big ass smile on her face.

The 9-1-1 call she made 2 hours later was bone chilling and so nonchalant that the dispatcher couldn't tell if the description of the situation was real or fake.

"Send somebody over here right now and get all of these dead ass thieves out of my motherfucking house, they're startin' to stink!!"

She was satisfied with her work and would gladly be taken away to pay for what she did. Deanna made sure all of her affairs were in order and although she knew that her daughter wasn't at the table, she made sure she left a note for her inside of the refrigerator.

THE BLACKEST BLUE

"Diane, too bad you couldn't make it for dinner, I saved some leftovers just for you!

P.S. I made your favorite banana pudding...If the cops don't get it, you can take it! Just like you all took my land!!"

Love,

Mama

Chapter 21

Colored Karma

A s the feather around the unit swirled in the tornado, it was known by officers and offenders that Old Lady Durham wasn't a breakfast person. Good luck to any idiot that decided to wake her up early. Lunch and dinner were her favorite meals…for obvious reasons. When she didn't wake up for lunch. The officer, who didn't bother to shake her or wake her for head count, is the same officer that didn't bother to wake her up for pill line either. Suddenly, late in the afternoon the officer realized that Old Lady Durham would never miss lunch and definitely not pill line. Durham was a diabetic. She didn't forget to wake Durham up because she didn't hear the supervisors repeat the *"live breathing body headcounts"* directive over and over a million times. She didn't bother because she didn't care for black and brown people...offenders or officers. She would only wake up white offenders for head count or if they were sleeping during chow and pill line calls. She blatantly showed favoritism to prisoners that were white. The amount of ignored grievances made her feel invincible, so trust me when I tell you, she never thought the day would come that she would have to explain herself. When Officer Holland flipped the covers back off of Old Lady Durham's face, she was as dead as her twenty -three relatives on Thanksgiving Day. Holland's scream could be heard all the way in the control room as she went into an immediate panic. She tried to think of an excuse as to why she falsified her early morning headcount. She checked the box with ink that Deanna Durham was alive and well at headcount. The cameras would tell the truth, she never even looked in her cell. She returned to the control room, knowing that her partner assigned to work with her was a black female. There would be a real problem in any attempt at a cover up story. In my heart and mind, she was the perfect person to eat a slice of colored karma pie. Simply because she was a racist, I tried to prove it before, MCCrae and countless other offenders filed grievances, and all of our complaints fell on deaf ears.

THE BLACKEST BLUE

I bet my life that if Old Lady Durham could make one last statement, she would laugh her ass off and say,

"I hope I scared your racist ass real good, cracker!"

I would have loved to have been a fly on the wall when Officer Holland had to explain to everyone in her chain of command, from all of the African American Sergeants, Lieutenants, Major and all the way up to the African American Warden, exactly why she didn't do a live breathing body headcount. Why she didn't wake Durham up for pill line or even check on Deanna Durham since the beginning of shift. According to the Medical Examiners, she was dead for over 6 hours.

It didn't take a lengthy investigation; Officer Holland was placed on administrative leave right then and there, but before she could get to her car, she was arrested. Charged with "Falsifying Documents, Dereliction of Duty and Official Oppression and anything else that would stick. After her arrest became public knowledge, Holland made multiple unsuccessful suicide attempts. I thought that she would be proud of herself and keep spewing her hate, the fact that she was ashamed made me question if she was really a racist and why she conducted herself like that at all if she's ashamed of being one.

I drove around the same block at least four times and thought that I was lost, but actually, I was on the back side of the Williamson County Sheriff's Office. Apparently, there were two different addresses in Google Maps. One side was where the training office was located and the other side was for the housing units, booking, medical, kitchen and the releasing area . I was greeted with a warm smile by Sergeant Winfree. He had a strong handshake and an inviting spirit. Grinning he said, *"Nice to finally put a face to a name."* Mainly because we had been in constant communication over the last 3 weeks. I passed everything with flying colors, but with each test that I took, there was someone else in charge of that portion of the hiring process. Our paths would only cross by email or on the phone.

He kept his word and kept tabs on my progress, making sure my file didn't sit on anyone's desk for more than 24 hours. I said, *"So, I finally get to meet the infamous Sergeant Winfree. I was starting to think you were a myth."* I said…looking at his name tag, "Ohhh I thought your last name was spelled like Oprah's with a Y. He said, "Nooo, Oprah's last name ends in a Y, like money…and mine ends in an E like broke." We both cracked up at that joke. I liked him, he had really good energy. He informed me that he was almost done with my background check and was in the process of calling my references. I was happy to hear that because working for TDCJ was mentally, physically, emotionally and spiritually…dehydrating.

I enjoyed the freedom of moving around the unit, and not having to work in the housing units, but after my 300th set of ass and tits, I was over it, especially the smell! I never got used to looking up into buttholes and vaginas all day, making sure they haven't shoved any stolen condiments in their "prison purse".

I got in the perimeter patrol car and went to the reception unit to turn in her personal affects and pick up the out-processing paperwork for Old Lady Durham. The reception unit housed offenders that were sentenced to prison, but were doing what I would consider "small time"… 3-5 years. They had 2 cages, one was for the newly sentenced, just coming into the system and the other cage was for the ones being released from prison. Unlike the movies, they don't just open the doors and let them out. Everyone will have to cross T's and dot I's. You definitely don't want to release anyone too early and you damn sure don't want to release the wrong person! I took the paper check from her commissary balance up there as well. They would eventually turn it over to her next of kin. I found that to be ironic. Even after her death, her family would still be taking something from her.

THE BLACKEST BLUE

The printout reflected that Denise Durham and a few other family members had been putting money on Deanna's books over the last 20 years. She had well over a hundred thousand dollars on her commissary and yet she never missed lunch and dinner.

She barely spent any of their money. *"Guilt money"* is what she had referred to it as. As I got to the last office on my list, an offender in the releasing cage asked if she could be let out to use the bathroom. I could see the officer was swamped and I said, *"I can escort whoever is asking for the bathroom if you're ok with it?"*

Officer McGilvery said, *"Oh lord, you're a saint, thank you, we are super busy today."*

She handed me the keys and I announced,

"Ok, ladies...who asked to go to the bathroom?"

A familiar voice said, "I did, Ma'am, will you take me for 75% off?"

Our eyes met, as I tried to contain my surprise when I said under my breath, *"Oh shit!"*

It was Tamika with the Big Body Benz from Lowe's!!

My eyes and my body spoke two different languages, I was cold and in officer mode...at first. I really wanted to hug her and tell her that I heard what happened but as fast as that thought came, so did reality...I knew Tamika for one week...4 ½ years ago. I really didn't know her at all, hell I still didn't know her last name!

As we walked to the bathroom, she said, "I always wondered if you got the job out here or if I would ever see you again one day." We kept walking and I said, *"Yep, I was hoping what they said about you wasn't true, but just so you know, your presence was missed at the store."*

She smiled, but I could tell that she was embarrassed more than anything.

"Hurry up, I need to be getting back to my unit." I said into the air, loud enough for anyone that was minding our business.

"You good, I didn't really have to pee, I knew you didn't see me, and I just wanted to get your attention, I am really sorry for how things turned out on your first day, I know they talked shit about me, I don't care, I still got my Benz though!" Tamika said. We both cracked up laughing like old times. She walked into the bathroom, washed her hands and walked right back out. We quickly walked back, and I locked her into the holding cage with the other prisoners. I wished her luck on her release and took the documents back to the

Administration building on Mountain View. *"Ahhh, just in time to do an escort with me to take Cell Block 3 to the chow hall."* Lieutenant Anderson said. I rolled my eyes behind his back, because he was on some bullshit, and I really didn't want no parts of it.

Chapter 22

Warning Signs

L ieutenant Tyrone Anderson was on the unit for about 11 years when he was transferred from the night shift to day shift. Late 40's, early 50's, his wife worked in the laundry department on the same unit. She was so excited about having similar hours as her husband. Normalcy was what they had both hoped for and although the new Major didn't care for me, he allowed the Anderson's to work the same hours in different departments. I met him a few times when I did overtime on night shift. His wife was a sweetheart, but he had a reputation as a hug-a-thug...a term we would label an officer that was too friendly with the prisoners. As soon as we stepped inside of Cell Block 2, Officer Harris pulled me aside. He was busy chit chatting with the offenders like they were old college buddies. He never noticed Harris talking to me.

Officer Harris began to walk in my direction. She entered the office behind me and whispered.

"Listen to me carefully, Lieutenant Anderson keeps coming down here to talk to and be around offender Willows, whatever you do, do not allow him to talk to her alone, he's been warned!"

And here goes the bullshit, I already knew I would be babysitting his ass as soon as I saw him.

*"How in the fuck am I going to tell a **Lieutenant** what offender he can and can't talk to??!!"* I asked her through gritted teeth and a low whisper. *"You're not telling him, Harris continued. Just kind of happen to get in the way of them being alone with Willows… how hard can that be?"*

Sarcastic was her tone, but really, she was just trying to look out for the brother. To be honest, we all were…but I learned early in this profession… you cannot save a person who keeps jumping in the deep end with weights around their ankles.

"Great, just what I need, a part-time babysitting job."

Now, I wish I had stayed my black ass in the kitchen because knowing what I knew, anything involving Lieutenant Anderson was going to give you a headache. I just didn't understand how his wife couldn't see how much he flirted with these convicts. It was like she didn't *want* to see it.

Harris wasn't laughing, she said, *"Tag, you're it! Watch out for his dumb ass, he's one of us!"*

Damn, did that mean one of us, as in an officer or one of us as in *"black"*. I felt sick to my stomach because I knew exactly what she meant when she said, "Tag, you're it".

"Damn it!"

There was an investigation going on, and more than likely, some shit was about to go down!

Now, I'm thinking, I got this! We're escorting 37 female offenders from a quarter of a mile away, how is he going to be alone with her?? I swear before I could even try to figure out how impossible that would be, I heard a loud, imitation of a wounded puppy moan, followed by an overdramatic *"Owwww!!!"*

It was offender Willows, clearly faking like she stepped on something and twisted her ankle. *"Go ahead and take the rest, I'll walk back here with her."* Lieutenant Anderson said, like he was so concerned for this wounded phony.

These sneaky motherfuckers! They had this planned all along, I thought.

"Nah, that's ok Sir, I'll walk with her, if you can take the rest of the group, we'll catch up to y'all at the chow hall."

I just knew I had ruined their secret plan when he barked, *"I said I got it, YOU go up front and escort the other offenders, I'll walk with her!"*

That was an order! I had never heard him address one of those convicted criminals like that but he damn sure put some base in his voice for me. I had to think quick! I stopped dead in my tracks and with a serious tone, I said, *"LT, let me holla at you."* Damn all of that tip-toeing, I figured I was just keep it real with him. As soon as he stepped to the side, he crossed his arms and he said, *"Yeah, what's up?"* Eyebrows scrunched together like he was irritated with me for taking him away from his woman. Ain't that some shit!

"LT, you know the policy, you can't be left alone with a female offender, without a female officer."

The way he looked at me, for wasting his time.

Oh, that's all you wanted?"

195

He sucked his teeth, waved me off, and walked right back towards Offender Willows.

I see why Officer Harris gave me that warning, Lieutenant Anderson was clearly forgetting that he had a wife. That she worked on this same unit, and he should know that once rumors get started, they were hard to stop. In other words, the way he was carrying on, Lieutenant Anderson was out of his rabbit ass mind! All the way to the chow hall and back, he stayed behind me and the other 36 offenders, while he walked and talked with Offender Willows like he was on a fucking date, strolling on the beach!

Officer Harris opened the door to 2 Block as we were getting closer to the entryway. She looked at how far behind they were in comparison to everyone else and shook her head.

Before I could explain, she said, *"It's not your fault, trust me ...we've all tried...Captain Hamlin and Major Fisher called, they said, don't go through the ODR when you come back to the kitchen, come in through the main doors."* I thought that was odd, but I followed the orders given.

Within two hours of my return to the kitchen, Lieutenant Anderson would be in handcuffs in the back of a patrol car, remembering that his wife worked on that same unit, realizing the strength of a rumor, wishing that he had listened to the countless officers that tried to save his ass. More than anything in the world, in that exact moment, he wished that he had saved himself from himself. Right after his love stroll with Offender Willows, he came into the **O**fficer's **D**ining **R**oom, pretending to be hungry. Well, he was, but not for food.

As if one offender wasn't enough, Lieutenant Anderson was playing a dangerous game with damaged goods. He took the bait set on the trap by Offender McClellan, Internal Affairs and Warden Chasen. Offender McClellan was sick and tired of having her heart broken. When the feather in the tornado landed in the ODR, she was devastated but she vowed that she wasn't going to be the only one crying around here!

She overheard two officers talking about Lieutenant Anderson and Offender Willows while working in the ODR one day. "E.T." as she affectionately called him, was aware of her case and promised that he would never mistreat her, all of the typical bullshit that you would expect him to say, he said it. Him leaving his wife was only a reality on one end of that forbidden relationship. Turns out, he was no better than Cody, worse if you asked her.

In her hurt and anger, she reported their relationship and everything that she heard about Lt. Anderson and Willows to Captain Hamlin. Warden Chasen set up a sting operation with prison officials and the FBI. They asked McClellan to wear a wire, and she agreed. The recording came through crystal clear as she asked if she could kiss him *"down there"*, but for a longer amount of time than the day before. He didn't confirm or deny a previous rendezvous, he just said, *"Ok baby"*.

His grey uniform pants were down to his ankles as he sat on the lid of the toilet in the bathroom stall. McClellan holding the sign he printed out months ago, marked *"Out of Order"* for their "personal time". *"Oh hell, I forgot the tape for the sign"* she lied, as she stepped out, leaving him naked from the waist down. When the door opened again, the agents had him fix his clothing before placing him in cuffs.

For three-hours, Lieutenant Anderson was interviewed. In total, 9 offenders were removed from different dorms on the unit. Each offender...a white female... was isolated and one by one, thoroughly interrogated. After each interview, the video along with their written statement was taken to an adjacent room where the warden, assistant warden and the major would make a folder attaching a picture of each victim with a S.A.N.E rape kit and a pregnancy test. You see, even if they were a willing participant, there's no such thing as consensual sex in the prison system, no matter who it's between. The weight of that entire process took a toll on everyone involved. After speaking with the Director of Prisons, a unanimous decision was made to have all 9 of the offenders transferred to other prisons all over Texas.

Tyrone Anderson was processed, fingerprinted and by morning, his mugshot made its way to the national news.

In 48 hours, he made one phone call … he called his mother.

He wanted to tell her before she could hear it from anywhere or anyone else. He knew when he was placed in cuffs that he had no intentions on calling his wife of 28 years. He reasoned that she could never understand the deep-rooted hatred that he had for white women. In his mind, she would think that he was fucking those white women because he would rather be with them, but that was far from the truth. He was attracted to his wife, he loved black women period. He hated white women deeply and would punish them sexually by holding their nose and shoving himself down their throat

At home he was a loving, thoughtful and a considerate husband.

But at work he would morph into a monster, a persona that would be considered nothing short of evil. Being taunted as a kid while growing up in Mississippi, he watched "them" lie on little black boys and do far worse to black men. He would make the women call him Mr. E.T., for his own sexually gratification. Years ago, when they were newlyweds, he and his wife watched the movie E.T. over and over, until they fell asleep. He would dress up as the extraterrestrial for Halloween and had a huge poster of E.T. on the wall behind his desk. His co-workers and family members bought him little E.T. figurines for Christmas. They lined the windowsill, his desk and all around his filing cabinet in his office.

Chapter 23

E.T. Plus Nine

The world knew about that little brown creature, with the blanket on his head in the basket of the bicycle. With nothing left to hide, he told investigators that there was no other way he would have been able to get away with making all of those white women call him *Mr. Emitt Till*, without their knowledge. His wife, an Afrocentric Godiva chocolate sister with natural hair and a voluptuous body, would never in a million years comprehend that her husband was sleeping with prisoners...their ethnicity, made it far more damaging and simply intolerable, as far as she was concerned. The truth made her physically ill.

THE BLACKEST BLUE

As she always does, Warden Chasen thought that it that it would be the right thing to do if she stopped by their home to speak with her officer, his wife, Mrs. Anderson in person.

Over piping hot tea, they spoke at length. Any questions that were asked, no matter how hurtful, the answer was provided. Although she didn't get any answers from him directly, she did get the closure that she needed. Warden Chasen hugged her and told her to take as much time as she needed before returning to work. Warden Chasen's empathy felt heroic in that moment. She did everything she could within the limits of her power to ease the immeasurable amount of pain. She even offered Officer Anderson an immediate transfer to a male unit. This way, if she didn't want to deal with the pressure of being on a female unit and the potential for gossip, she didn't have to. With sad puppy dog eyes, she told Warden Chasen, *"Let me think it over, I'll call you in a few days."* That was the most reasonable response she could mentally process. Satisfied with that answer, Warden Chasen nodded, said a little prayer out loud let herself out.

Mrs. Anderson got up from the fetal position that she was in for most of the warden's visit and began to strategically walk through her own home. Instantly looking at the décor through a new set of eyes. Believing she missed countless clues, she began to look at everything, through *his* eyes.

There were framed photographs of Malcom X and Martin Luther King Jr. in his home office and not one image of E.T. anywhere. Vibrant and colorful poems and pictures of actresses, singers, dancers and powerful politicians from the 60's. There were no Western Union receipts, written love letters or anything that would show that he did anything for these women financially. Not an inkling that he cared about any of them.

She looked through his desk, checked his computer history and even emptied out his work bag, nothing, not even condoms. And just like that...it hit her.

He was having unprotected sex with them, all of them...all nine of them, raw! He had to have been, she reasoned with herself. They must have told the warden and investigators that he wasn't using protection. She didn't even think to ask Warden Chasen about condoms. It all made logical sense, the pregnancy tests, transferring all of them right away. The thought of any of them possibly being pregnant didn't sit right in her heart, even if they were black. She couldn't have children herself; early cervical cancer ended that possibility. *"What if they were all pregnant?"* The thought ran through her head so fast it made her dizzy, she lifted the trash can up from the floor in his office and began to vomit.

All night, she tossed and turned in their marital bed, humiliated, embarrassed, ashamed and alone. In the morning, after her coffee…for breakfast, she ate her gun.

I remembered where I put his business card, and it made me smile when he remembered me every single time I called. *"Hey Brooklyn, I know that voice anywhere!"* Sergeant Yardly would say. We stayed in touch over the years, and he had my undivided attention when offering advice about my career. I disclosed my plans to go to The Williamson County Sheriff's Office, and although he wished I was going to work at his police department, he was still proud of me for making the career change. He had made a career change himself, with so much time on the clock he was now in charge of the Explorer Program for the police department. He worked with the youth, ages 14-18, training them to become police officers, assist in parades and just being an awesome mentor to them. I asked him about Sergeant Murillo, and he corrected me as he loudly cleared his throat, *"Lieutenant Murillo is doing very well for herself!"*

"Ohhh wow, tell her congrats for me please." I'm always proud when a female advances in this kind of career. Her ethnicity doesn't matter because believe it or not WOMEN have it hard in this male dominating field, but a black or brown woman is on difficulty level 10! God forbid if they

have an alternative lifestyle, they're in a class all by themselves in the mistreatment department. Sergeant Yardly and I shared texts during the process, and he remained positive without hesitation when I would vent to him about any and everything.

I quietly turned in my 2 weeks' notice to H.R.; I literally kept my mouth shut about leaving because the officers were oftentimes worse than the prisoners with the gossiping.

I didn't want to tell anyone that I would be quitting because I've watched my colleagues do some evil shit out of jealousy. The way I had mapped it out, I had a few more working days at Mountain View until my last day. The plan was to sit at home relaxing and getting things in order for three whole weeks before my start date at Wilco. I was supposed to start on November 15th and I tell you no lie, I couldn't wait to turn in those dusty grey, crooked ass blue striped, ill-fitting uniforms that didn't compliment anyone's complexion.

Now I have been on the unit long enough to know when the energy is off with certain people. It was a Monday, and this energy was different in a weird way. For some odd reason, Major Fisher was acting like nothing ever happened. He spoke when he came into the kitchen like we were cool, and the issue with him trying to suspend me for not signing that last write up miraculously didn't exist. He didn't try to give me a dap, because he knew I would leave his fist hanging, just like I did that pen. I was really beginning to think that he was bipolar. He was so night and day, hot and cold and I didn't trust his ass as far as I could see him.

All I had to do was make it through 10 working days and I was outta here!

Not long after I got to work, Captain Hamlin asked me if I could come in for 1st shift the following day and I agreed but that would mean I would have to go right back home because that shift starts at 2am. No one knew I was coming in at that hour, except the two of us. Mainly because he was considering shuffling the deck for the officers.

Now I'll be honest, I was told that the morning shift supervisor was a stone hearted bitch when you work with her. The entire two years in the kitchen, she was cordial, but we were always like two ships in the night. Once our shift showed up, we transferred and documented keys and knives...but we only spent about an hour in the kitchen at the same time before first shift left for the day.

Chapter 24

Checkmate

I didn't want to judge her, so as far as I was concerned…her slate was clean with me. I just did my job and really tried not to get in her way. Not just because she was an older feisty German woman…but because everyone on the unit knew that she was OCD and ran shit with an iron fist. I was already on the Major's shit list; I didn't need anything else to happen. Nine working days!

The morning went smooth, caught a few kitchen workers doing dumb shit and wrote one up, but other than that, it was really uneventful. Ms. Vogle was a workhorse, she stayed busy and I did what I would have done on 2nd shift…we had no issues, especially with each other.

That was until my actual shift arrived. My co-workers were not aware that I was already here on shift and for some reason, that ticked Ms. Washington the fuck off. To this day, I still don't know why. Almost as if nobody ran my schedule change by her for approval.

In hindsight, I found that people were territorial in this line of work. Maybe she felt like because she used to work on first shift, if they needed help, it should have been offered to her first. Who knows?? Your guess is as good as mine.

All I knew was that I was glad I would be getting off early. It was my Friday, and not only would I be off by 10am, but I would also be off for the next 3 days after that. I took that long ass walk from the kitchen to my car and as soon as I sat down in the driver's seat, I saw two K-9 officers in the parking lot. Now usually they go around the officer's cars, the dumpsters and the officer's barracks. I sat there texting on my phone and being nosey.

After there are no alerts, they usually walk around the perimeter of the super maximum unit and that's it.

Unless there is a report or an incident that sounds like drugs may have been involved, they don't bring the dogs into the unit. Outside around the parking lot and around the barracks is basically the extent of the K-9 search.

The ranking supervisors park in a different area altogether. The way that the fence is built, their parking area it's off to the side of the unit. Away from the peasant officer's parking lot. They park in a *"we're the almighty"* patch of grass.

While the ranking officials were out in the parking lot catching up on old times with the senior K-9 handler, none of them noticed the rookie K-9 handler, who wasn't aware of the *"routine"* route, walk with the dog to where he saw "other cars", completely unaware that those *elite* vehicles were not to be searched…**ever!**

To everyone's surprise the dog started barking and sat in front of a car….the fucking K-9 hit on Major Fisher's car!

Good for that Motherfucker!!

The euphoric part was, I was right there to see it all go down for myself and didn't need to get the story second hand.

All I could say to myself was *"that explains everything"*. When you fuck with that *"Booger Sugar"* you're liable to act an ass for no reason.

Look at God!

Knowing that he wouldn't be there when I got back to work was a relief in itself. Aware that his fall from his high horse was not cushioned in any way, sat well within my soul. It crossed my mind to ask the warden, *"Hey Ma'am, now that we all know Major Fisher was probably high when he set his sites on me...you think maybe we should throw those write ups out?"* Then I thought.... eh, too soon.

Little did I know, none of those write ups would matter anymore, because after 3 ½ days off, my first day back to work would be my last day, *period!*

Hair, nails and eyebrows freshly done. I was well-rested and entering work with the best kept secret, I had 8 working days to go. When Ms. Washington let the gate close behind her instead of holding it for me, the tone was set for the day, here we go again with the bipolar bullshit. Is she still mad from last week? This lady need medication...damn!

Unbeknownst to all of us officers, Captain Hamlin switched the 1st and 2nd shift supervisors on the schedule so when we came in for 2nd shift, Ms. German OCD herself was busy at work and barking orders. My poker face practice came in handy, and since we worked together without an issue the last time...today should be cool too ...I hoped. I usually sit at the same table with the other officers but after that gate closed in my face earlier, I kept my distance. My plan was to make sure that I stayed busy for the hour before the other shift was off the clock. I saw what was on the menu for dinner and after we pat searched our crew of offenders in, I would start prepping.

THE BLACKEST BLUE

In my own zone and out of anyone's way, I did a little recon in the stock rooms to see where all of the ingredients to make patty melts were. This wasn't unusual, but I really wanted to pass time because I was annoyed. Now as we exit the kitchen to receive our workers, I do a little small talk with Officer King, really just as a temperature check, but she was good with me.

So now I'm positive that the shit with Ms. Washington is personal and I'm convinced that Ms. King don't do the bandwagon bullshit. That honestly made me feel better about the energy I was feeling. As Ms. King and I were chit chatting and laughing, out of my peripheral, I see Ms. Washington's face scrunched all the way up like she smelled shit. It was like the sound of my voice made her sick or something. The last offender was pat searched and as we do every single day, we walk up the three steps and through the entrance door of the kitchen. Ms. King went first and then Ms. Washington. My Brooklyn mentality was *" ain't no way I'm letting you walk behind me and you acting funny",* so I walked behind *her.* As she got to the second step, Ms. Washington stopped dead in her tracks, stretched her arms out like Jesus on the cross and grabbed the handrails on each side, blocking me from entering the kitchen. For no reason whatsoever, this lunatic looked over her shoulder and said to me, *"Now what are you going to do?"* I just looked at her and went around to the stairs leading to the exit door and entered in through that way. She stood there and watched me walk in and thennnnnn she came in the kitchen. Now there are a few things that was happening in that moment, I had to process that there were no cameras out there, she didn't say that bullshit loud enough for anyone to hear and she was 15-20 years my senior. I really had to take that "L" because one thing for sure, working in law enforcement, they have no problem with locking your ass up when you commit a crime! I knew she was trying to wake "Brooklyn" up and I was just trying to get through these last few days.

Now remember, I was already staying the fuck away from this lady, but I guess ignoring her made her even angrier. I was heated but I already had it in my mind to get a few of the kitchen workers together and start on the prep for patty melts. Within 30 minutes of the shifts changing out, the lunch line was in full swing, and everyone was busy. It takes about an hour and a half to serve everyone on the unit, in that cafeteria style setting. Don't forget, we still have to take tray carts to Death Row, Administrative Segregation and Cell block 1 and Cell Block 2. With them, we usually wait about 45 minutes before picking the carts up again, but they also eat before everyone else. So, now follow along as I break down how the bullshit took a hard left. While lunch is being served, the dinner meal is either being pulled off of the shelf or prepped to cook. Depending on how much work it takes to make what's on the menu. Anybody in their right mind would tell you that all 600 offenders are entitled to 2 patty melts each and that's quick math, even for a 5th grader. For the 2 years that I have already been in the kitchen, this was the most tedious meal to prep for. This was the meal that you would start early because of the prep work. You'll need no less than a team of 5-6 kitchen workers to form an assembly line in order to execute this prep efficiently.

So, I did just that....

Hamburger patties were lined up like soldiers in formation on the cookie sheet.

Rolled out the butcher paper, the entire length of the steel table. Got 2 workers holding a loaf of bread, I had the cheese, of course. Cheese is like gold in a prison. Everybody was in position so that we can make this happen smoothly.

We knocked out 2 trays in less than 15 minutes. I mean we had a nice little operation going on when the door swung open and there was Ms. *"Getting' On My Motherfucking Nerves"* Washington in the flesh.

To this day, I imagined that she looked around and saw I wasn't around to fuck with, because she came in the door like she was looking for *me*. She walked right over and looked down at the table with her hands on her hips and said, *"Hmmp."* Not loud, but loud enough for me to hear her, just like she did with that weird ass comment outside. Exactly like these convicts do, because usually the one that's making the most noise is considered the aggressor. That's a nasty trait she picked up, but I'm no fool. I paid her no mind and kept on working. The smug look on her face was a cross between, *"Oh that's a smart way to do that and I wish I would have thought to do it that way!"*

Either way, she didn't say anything directly to me and after her inspection was complete, instead of going through the door she entered from, she went through the door that connects to the serving line. I already knew Messy Bessy was going to start some unnecessary shit.

Within seconds, and I do mean seconds...Ms. Vogle came through the serving line door like a raging bull on steroids in a china store!

Not, *"Oh, thank you for getting that started for me."* No kudos for being proactive. Instead, at the top of her voice in front of the 6 kitchen workers that were with me, I got,

"Who the hell told you to do that??!! Take it all apart and put it back!!"

So first, let's start with the fact that, this bitch is cursing at me and acting like I'm her child...for two she didn't have enough professionalism to ask me to step in the office. She was on the serving line, completely oblivious that she needed to be angry with anything at that moment.

For three, *whatever* Washington said to her, had her already pissed off as she walked through the door. I called myself helping and staying out of the way.

I promise, had the shift supervisors that are normally on 2nd shift been on duty, they would have been happy as hell that someone got that meal started, because it's tedious to say the least. I said, *"What do you mean, put it back? It's patty melts for dinner, we can't take these apart!"* The look on my face is like *"What the fuck idiotic demand is that?"*

That's literally like someone saying to put the peanut butter and jelly back in the jar after you made the sandwich.

Do you know that this, 4-foot 11 dictator picked up both of those cookie sheets and flung all of that shit in the trash right then and there! It had to be at least 60 pre-made patty melts and we needed more than 1,200! The workers just stood there waiting for the next move… and it was on me.

I thought *"checkmate bitch, watch this."*

I went in the office, sat the cheese on the desk, grabbed my jacket and walked out. The offenders knew I was up to something, but I didn't say a word.

I bet my life that Ms. Vogle and Ms. Washington thought that I was taking a break and would be right back or crying to somebody…shitttt I wasn't headed to anywhere but the Human Resources building. I told Ms. Cortez, *"Make my resignation effective right fucking now, before I fuck them bitches up in that kitchen!"*

She jumped from her chair screaming, *"Wait, wait!!! Let me get somebody down here to talk to you."* My mind was already made up and *"Brooklyn was wide awake."*

I had only been living in Texas for 5 years at this point and I wasn't as knowledgeable with how the law worked like I am now.

What I did know was that, if I beat Ms. Washington's ass, I am going to blow my career at Williamson County. So, with every encounter, instead of being a hot head and flipping shit over.

I just let them believe that they were winning. I had bigger and better fish to fry. I could hear Ms. Cortez on the phone telling somebody, *"You better get down here, she's about to walk out!"*

I was removing my keys from the key clip, my radio and mace from the holsters. As Lieutenant Wilson walked in the office, our eyes locked.

She knew. She's a black female...she knew!

I didn't have to say it. But she had to give it a shot so that she can say, *"I tried."*

"What will it take for you to go back to work today?" she asked me, concerned that I didn't have a plan B.

"A police escort! Because if I go back in that kitchen, I'm going to get locked up for fucking up Ms. Washington and Ms. Vogle...is that what you want?" I put the keys and the radio in her hands as Ms. Cortez was calling Captain Hamlin. I walked towards the door and told Ms. Cortez, *"Calling him is pointless, if he had a spine, half of the shit that goes on in that kitchen, wouldn't! I'll be in touch to turn in my uniforms."* I opened the door and walked out. I giggled my ass off as I thought about the fact that Ms. King was leaving early today, and it would just be the two miserable bitches

doing all of that work, especially on patty melt day. Serves them right...and like I thought earlier...**CHECKMATE!!**

As we were walking towards the front gate, she said she understood my frustration, Lieutenant Wilson was listening closely as I told her about starting at Wilco, the pay and the hours. The entry door to Death Row swung open and Melinda McCarty was being escorted to a visit by two officers and a Sergeant. I really wish they would go ahead and roll up her sleeve already but knowing I would never have to deal with her evil ass again was fine by me.

As I entered the front gate area, there was a black man with his back turned to me. I figured this must be McCarty's son handing in his ID to visit his momster. But when he turned around, our eyes locked and I didn't even try to stop the words that deliberately came from my mouth, *"Nate? Franny Newt's man, up here to see McCarty! Now that's fucked up!!*

He just put his head down, there was nothing he could say.

I wished it wasn't my last day, because I would have exposed that wicked witch to the other ladies on the Row. I was so glad that Newt didn't marry his sorry ass! He had the look of instant regret on his face as soon as he saw me. The sad thing was, no one knows if this was his first or his tenth visit.

But I'm sure Franny Newt was turning in her grave, for more reason than one! As the gate closed behind me for the final time…I felt free like I had just made parole. Williamson County…here I come!

Blacker Than Blue: First Impressions

I swear, if I didn't have bad luck…I would have no luck at all! Two days before I started, I did a test drive to the Williamson County Jail. I just wanted to gauge the drive, the traffic and how long it would take. No issues, there and back. The road through the town of Florence reminded me of that old town from the movie "Cars". It's a one-horse town, one little gas station, one traffic light and fields and fields of grass. At 4PM…it looks deserted…so imagine at 4AM! As luck would have it, on my first day …my black ass caught a flat in the middle on nowhere! I was too scared to sit there and too scared to keep driving on the flat. Sheriff's uniform on or not…I was not about to be found swinging from a tree! I can replace that tire and that rim….so yeah you guessed it…I put my flashers on and drove 3 miles an hour…for 25 minutes. As crazy as that seems, I made it to work early, even before some of the other officers. Sgt. Jameson said, *"Don't ever ride on a flat like that, you should have called."* I responded with, *" On my first day?? No Ma'am, first impressions are everything!* She agreed and waited outside with me for USAA to tow my car directly to Discount Tires. Standing out there, getting to know me and giving me a ride when my car was ready, really made me feel like the supervisors at Williamson County cared for their officer's way more than the supervisors at TDCJ…but I couldn't have been more wrong in my whole life. Sergeant Jameson was a wolf in sheep's clothing. First impressions my ass! I thought she would be inspiring. I thought she would have that "from one black woman to another" kind of mentality. That couldn't be further from the truth and once again…it's always my **own**!

About the Author

S.D Epps was born and raised in the face-moving, always hustling, diverse neighborhood of Brownsville in Brooklyn, New York. Growing up, she developed a strong sense of justice and an unyielding determination to make a difference. This passion led her to serve in the United States Army on active duty and then to pursue a career in law enforcement, specifically within the field of corrections.

With an illustrious career spanning over 25 years, she has dedicated her life to maintaining order, ensuring safety, and advocating for the rights and rehabilitation of incarcerated youth at the Department of Juvenile Justice in NYC, Women's Death Row at the Mt. View Unit with TDCJ. Her journey took her to the Williamson County Jail, where she worked tirelessly, earning the respect and admiration of her colleagues and inmates alike. Through perseverance and unwavering commitment, she was the first black person, male or female to test and promote to the rank of Lieutenant, becoming a trailblazer and a role model for many. Her journey at the Travis County Sherif's Office, although it was brief, it was where she retired from and will forever hold a place in her heart.

Her experiences as a woman of color in law enforcement has placed her in unique situations, unfortunate circumstances and many moments of clarity, some of which she passionately shares through her writing. In her autobiographical novel, she delves deep into the challenges, triumphs, and nuances of working in a women's prison, offering readers an unfiltered glimpse into the world of corrections from a perspective often underrepresented.

S.D. Epps continues to reside in Texas physically, but Brooklyn will always be home. When she's not writing, she's enjoying her retirement with her family and friends, traveling and exploring new avenues to inspire and uplift those around her.

Meet the Author

Other books by the Author:

(1) My Daddy is in Jail (Published 2024)

(2) My Mommy is in Jail

TBD (2025)

(3) Blacker Than Blue

TBD (2025-2026)

(4) My Black is Not My Blues…
TBD (2026-2027).

Daddy, Grandma Helene', Daddy Joe, Momma Les, Momma Bessie Mae, Uncle Mike and Auntie Bev, Taneisha, Joseph, Gregory, T'Kai and my childhood friends Crystal, Shakeia & LaTisha...

I love you all with my whole heart...
Sleep in Peace.
Always Loved, Never Forgotten

www.ingramcontent.com/pod-product-compliance
Lightning Source LLC
Chambersburg PA
CBHW071727120626